# IMPLEMENTING CANADA'S DEFENCE POLICY STATEMENT

## The Canadian Institute of Strategic Studies

*Chairman of the Board of Directors: MGen (Retd) D. Fraser Holman, CD*
*President and Executive Director: David Rudd*
*Research Officer: Deborah Bayley*

The Canadian Institute of Strategic Studies provides the forum for, and is a vehicle to stimulate the research, study, analysis, and discussion of the strategic implications of major national and international issues, events and trends as the they affect Canada and Canadians.

The CISS is currently working independently or in conjunction with other organizations in a variety of fields including counter-terrorism; Canadian security and soveriegnty; arms control and disarmament; Canada-US security cooperation and; defence transformation.

### CISS PUBLICATIONS INCLUDE:

FREE WITH MEMBERSHIP:
- Spring/Fall Seminar Proceedings
- Strategic Datalinks
- Strategic Profile: Canada
- The CISS Bulletin
- Canadian Military Journal/Revue Militare Canadienne

The CISS is an independent, non-profit organization.
For membership, seminar, and publications information contact:

The Canadian Institute of Strategic Studies
165 University Avenue, Suite 702
Toronto, Ontario, M5H 3B8
Tel: (416) 322-8128 Fax: (416) 322-8129
E-mail: info@ciss.ca
http://www.ciss.ca

# IMPLEMENTING CANADA'S DEFENCE POLICY STATEMENT

EDITED BY
DAVID RUDD
DEBORAH BAYLEY
KAREN EVERETT

 THE CANADIAN INSTITUTE OF STRATEGIC STUDIES

Library and Archives Canada Cataloguing in Publication

The Canadian Institute of Strategic Studies.
Spring Seminar (2005: Toronto, Ont.)
Copyright 2005

Implementing Canada's Defence Policy Statement
edited by David Rudd, Deborah Bayley, Karen Everett.

Proceedings of the Canadian Institute of Strategic Studies
Spring Seminar, held in Toronto, Ont., July 22, 2005.
ISBN 1-894736-10-9

1. Canada--Defenses--Congresses. I. Rudd, David II. Bayley, Deborah III. Everett, Karen
IV. Title.

UA600.C364 2005          355'.033071          C2005-906479-X

# TABLE OF CONTENTS

Glossary ..................................................................................................vi

Opening Remarks ..................................................................................1
*David Rudd*

Has Canada Awoken? ............................................................................5
*Andrew Cohen*

Making Inter-departmental 'Jointness'(3-D) Work ...............................12
*Mark Sedra*

The New Defence Agenda ...................................................................23
*Dr. Douglas Bland*

Son of Global Mobile:
The Historical Origins of the Defence Policy ......................................29
*Dr. Sean Maloney*

Question and Answer Forum ...............................................................38

The Procurement Cycle's Race
with Obsolescence 1960-2005 .............................................................46
*General (Retd) Paul Manson*

Missing in Action: A Defence-Industrial
Strategy for Canada .............................................................................54
*Peter Boag*

Setting Our Course ..............................................................................65
*General R. J. Hillier*

Question and Answer Forum ...............................................................75

# Glossary

| | |
|---|---|
| 3-D | Defence, Development and Diplomacy |
| ACE | Allied Command Europe |
| AIAC | Aerospace Industries Association of Canada |
| ADM-HR Mil | Assistant Deputy Minister Human Resources (Military) |
| BMD | Ballistic Missile Defence |
| CANCOM | Canada Command |
| CAP | Canadian Aerospace Partnership |
| CC | Canadian Cargo |
| CCL | Commerce Control List |
| CDA | Conference of Defence Associations |
| CDS | Chief of Defence Staff |
| CEFCOM | Canadian Expeditionary Forces Command |
| CF | Canadian Forces |
| CFP | Canada's Frigate Patrol |
| CIBG | Canadian Infantry Brigade Group |
| CIDA | Canadian International Development Agency |
| CIIA | Canadian Institute of International Affairs |
| CIMIC | Civil-Military Cooperation |
| CISS | Canadian Institute of Strategic Studies |
| CLO | Conduct of Land Operations |
| DCDS | Deputy Chief of the Defence Staff |
| DDH | Designated Destroyer Helicopter |
| DDSA | Defence Development Sharing Arrangements |
| DoD | Department of Defense |
| DND | Department of National Defence |
| DPS | Defence Policy Statement |
| DPSA | Defence Production Sharing Arrangements |
| DRDC | Defence Research and Development Canada |
| EU | European Union |
| FAC | Foreign Affairs Canada |
| FMC | Forces Mobile Command |
| GDP | Gross Domestic Product |
| HMCS | Her Majesty's Canadian Ship |
| IOC | Initial Operational Capability |
| IPS | International Policy Statement |
| IS | Internal Security |
| ISAF | International Security Assistance Force |
| ITAR | International Traffic in Arms Regulations |
| IRB | Industrial Regional Benefits |
| JTF-2 | Joint Task Force 2 |
| L-20 | Leaders of 20 leading countires |
| LAV | Light Armoured Vehicle |

| | |
|---|---|
| MCP | Major Crown Project |
| MHP | Maritime Helicopter Project |
| NAFTA | North American Free Trade Agreement |
| NATO | North Atlantic Treaty Organization |
| NCM | Non-Commisioned Member |
| NCO | Non-Commisioned Officer |
| NDHQ | National Defence Headquarters |
| NORAD | North American Aerospace Defence Command |
| NGO | Non-Governmental Organization |
| NSA | New Shipborne Aircraft |
| NSH | New SAR Helicopter |
| OECD | Organization for Economic Cooperation and Developmnet |
| OTC | Officer Training Corps |
| PJBD | Permanent Joint Board on Defence |
| PK | Peacekeeping |
| PRT | Provincial Reconstruction Team |
| R&D | Research and Development |
| RCAF | Royal Canadian Air Force |
| RFP | Request for Proposal |
| RMC | Royal Military College of Canada |
| SAR | Search and Rescue |
| SFOR | Stabilisation Force (Bosnia-Herzegovina) |
| SOG | Special Operations Group |
| TCCCS | Tactical Command and Control Communications System |
| TRUMP | Tribal Class Update and Modernization Project |
| UH | Utility Helicopter |
| UN | United Nations |
| UNEF | United Nations Emergency Force |
| US | United States |
| VTOL | Vertical Take-Off and Landing |
| WTO | World Trade Organization |

# OPENING REMARKS

## David Rudd

Twice each year the Canadian Institute of Strategic Studies gathers together a group of analysts to explore an issue of particular strategic importance to Canada. This particular event, "Implementing Canada's Defence Policy Statement", is intended to re-introduce the public to the work that has been done so far to put Canada's defence and security on a sounder footing, and to assess the likelihood that the work will continue.

I use the word "re-introduce" deliberately. Many Canadians will only vaguely recall the release of the Defence Policy Statement (DPS) in April of 2005. It quickly disappeared from the headlines. One also senses that wider and sustained public interest in the policy statement was not forthcoming because the Government of Canada had previously announced a major cash infusion for defence to the tune of $12.8-billion over the next five fiscal years. This was itself upstaged by the near-simultaneous announcement that Canada would not officially take part in the US continental missile defence shield.

Since April we have begun to see evidence that the transformation of Canada's defence effort is more than just declaratory policy. The military command structure is being overhauled so that domestic operations can be carried off more seamlessly. The Chief of Defence Staff and his senior planners have met in Cornwall, Ontario to begin putting meat on the policy bone. The individual services are striving to think and act jointly. A general sense of optimism prevails - as it should, for this is what one would normally expect from the senior ranks and from the Minister's office.

---

**David Rudd** is the President and Executive Director of the Canadian Institute of Strategic Studies.

And yet alongside the general consensus that the policy goals outlined in the defence statement, and in the larger International Policy Statement (IPS) are quite reasonable, one senses a growing scepticism - at least among the members of the defence analytic community - that the promised resources will indeed be forthcoming, or that the government's interest in real transformation is sustainable.

I imagine that this stems as much from the realization that policy statements are essentially promissory notes as it does from a well-founded belief that we have been here before. The defence white papers of 1987 and 1994 laid out objectives that were ultimately not met. Throughout the 1990s resource scarcity was coupled with the over-deployment of the Canadian Forces, leading to an increasingly dysfunctional defence effort that the government, to its credit, finally (and formally) recognized.

Scepticism surrounds everything from the timely delivery of new kit to the recruitment of up to 5,000 extra regular force personnel and 3,000 reservists over the next five years. These are necessary but extremely ambitious goals, and one wonders if a combination of bureaucracy, economic uncertainty, and the usual vagaries of politics will defeat these intentions. Although there was no opposition in parliament to either the policy statement or the additional appropriations, a lengthy parliamentary minority may oblige the government to continue buying the support and goodwill of other parties, thereby leaving less room at budget time for defence transformation. Even in the age of global terrorism there will be no domestic political price to pay if the promised enhancements to the CF's expeditionary capabilities do not materialize. And unless a major natural catastrophe should befall us, military unpreparedness will likewise not be punished at the polls.

Scepticism also stems from the implicit assumptions in the DPS. Among these are that failed states breed terrorism, and should be the centre of our attention; that traditional combat will be a rarity, and; that we have a responsibility to protect vulnerable populations. How solid are these assumptions?

Most suicide bombers, including those of 9/11 and 7/7 infamy, do not come from failed states. Indeed, many states either fail or exist in a state of fragility without directly affecting the security of Canada and Canadians. Think of the Balkans, which consumed political attention and resources throughout the 1990s. Think of East Timor. Is there indeed a link between state failure and Canadian security in all cases? In some cases? If so, which ones? Do the International and Defence Policy Statements help us come to grips with these issues?

The notion that state versus state conflict is on the wane is a fashionable notion that may yet prove to be wrong. But what is known is that Canada's expeditionary force goals, dating from the 1994 White Paper, have been reduced dramatically by the current DPS. We have dropped the "commitment" to deploy an army brigade and a wing of fighter aircraft, while the navy will soon lose the ability to form a task group. Some will argue that the nature of conflict has irrevocably changed, and that mass is no longer an issue. But even modern peace support operations can, over time, eat up huge amounts of personnel and equipment. So because quantity has a quality all its own, the force reductions mentioned above are a tacit admission that Canada will no longer seek a position of genuine influence within an allied coalition by deploying a critical mass of combat forces. To be sure, we will seek and be given positions of responsibility. But influence is another matter.

Of course Canada may resolve this problem simply by choosing to stay out of state-on-state conflicts just as it stayed out of Iraq. But successive governments often make foreign and defence policy decisions on the fly. They develop criteria for our military deployments and then fail to observe those criteria. The future is therefore unknown. But as Andrew Cohen has pointed out, our diminishing ability to influence that future is known. And it may take 20 years to put things right.

In the meantime we have embarked on a grand philanthropic exercise that is intended to give hope to millions who suffer from the wilful neglect of their governments. *The Responsibility to Protect* has been promoted at the United Nations as a way of ameliorating the effects of state repression or failure, even if it requires encroaching on the sovereignty of target countries. The concept has been praised by liberals in the developed world, but pilloried in much of the developing world as neo-colonialism. What is germane to this discussion is that Canada's support for the concept could see it pulled militarily, diplomatically, economically into so many regions of the world for indefinite periods of time. How do the various policy statements intend to cope with this possibility? Or will the commitment be exposed as merely rhetorical? After all, there was no rush to do anything about Darfur, nor Rwanda before it.

The point is that the DPS, like the larger International Policy Statement, provokes as many questions as it answers. It may indeed be a sound blueprint for the future, but it is based on assumptions that may or may not prove to have longevity. As Colonel Howie Marsh pointed out in a recent essay on the history of defence policy-making, Canadian governments have got it wrong six out of the last seven times!

Those attending these proceedings may have done so with the expectation that they would be treated to a presentation on what the DPS and IPS might mean for the US-Canada security relationship. This is an important topic to be sure, but it occurred to us that we could have a serious conversation about Canada's defence and security without getting side-tracked by how Washington will react to what Ottawa is proposing. In a recent panel discussion in Calgary I tried to preempt any extraneous debate on the bilateral relationship, knowing that at least some in the audience would be inclined to look at Canada's defence effort through the lens of contemporary US foreign policy; that we should have nothing to do militarily with those 'perfidious' Yanks so long as Mr. Bush is on the throne.

I was at pains to point out that what the Americans are up to is to a large extent irrelevant. The DPS is a "made in Canada" document and although it deals with international security partnerships it is up to Canadians to determine what type of defence and security effort they want to have. It is the merits and demerits of the DPS that should concern us. What our allies are doing is of secondary importance. Our defence and international security policies would exist in some form regardless of who is sitting in the White House. If we make up our minds as to what is at stake both at home and abroad and what absolutely must be done about it, if we get the big things right, then all else should fall into place.

Or so one hopes. Strategic thought is not generally part of a Canadian government's political calculus. Electoral fortunes command greater attention than whether we show a visible presence on the international stage. Visibility is an elastic term, and in any case is not derived solely from our defence effort. Future governments may choose to contribute police or development assistance to some far-away crisis, and leave the troops at home.

# Has Canada Awoken?

## Andrew Cohen

My central question today is: after decades of decline in the world, after a generation of slumber, has Canada awoken?

In his memoirs, Charles de Gaulle memorably said: "All my life I have had a certain idea of France." Now think about that for a moment: an idea of France. The power of that statement is arresting. It's so full of pride and possibility. There is a sense of the nation, a sense of its purpose. Of course, General de Gaulle did have that idea of France and there is no doubt that his countrymen did as well. No one could accuse them of being shy about their society or their history, their contribution to art, literature and philosophy, indeed to much of western civilization. It is no surprise that they would think of themselves in the world in terms of a *project de société*. It suggests a kind of a national mission, a purpose, something a people want to do in the world.

And that same sense of confidence can be found, I would argue, in the Americans, the British, the Russians, the Chinese, and the Israelis. In fact, you can find it in any great people with a history of achievement. The Romans understood it when they boasted, *Civis Romanus sum* ("I am a citizen of Rome"). John F. Kennedy understood it when he went to Berlin in 1963 and said *Ich bin ein Berliner* ("I am a citizen of Berlin"). In both cases, the idea of citizenship -- in the first instance of a great empire, in the second as part of a free city surrounded by Communism -- reflected a pride in belonging to something meaningful and bigger than themselves.

Yet when it comes to Canada, or more precisely Canada in the world, we do not

---

**Andrew Cohen** is an Associate Professor at the Carleton University School of Journalism and author of *While Canada Slept: How We Lost Our Place in the World* (McClelland & Stewart, 2003).

have that same sense of confidence as other peoples, even those younger, smaller, poorer, and less successful than we. I suggest that we are still searching for that idea of ourselves abroad, and we will not have truly awakened until we find it.

Two generations ago we had that idea of ourselves. We were a warrior doing what we thought we had to do in the world. We emerged with the fourth-largest military in the world in 1945, having fought successfully on land, air and sea. Later we were the world's leading peacekeeper, scarcely refusing a mission between the 1950s and the late 1980s. We contributed 10 percent of the world's peacekeepers. We trained and led them and it became part of our national iconography. It was not all that we did, but we certainly fell in love with that sense of ourselves, which wasn't so bad because at least it was an idea of ourselves.

We were also, for a time, a social worker to the world. We were there in Colombo, Ceylon in 1950 when Lester Pearson established the world's first aid program to the developing world. We were there in 1969 when Mr. Pearson helped establish 0.7 percent of gross domestic product as an international standard measure of aid. We never did what we said we would in terms of contributing that share of our national wealth, but we did more than we do now.

We had other ideas of ourselves. We were the world's diplomat, its honest broker and helpful fixer in the middle decades of the 20th century in what became known as the "Golden Age of Canadian Diplomacy." As a builder we helped to create much of the architecture after the Second World War: the United Nations, the General Agreement on Tariffs and Trade, the World Bank, the International Monetary Fund, the North Atlantic Treaty Organization, and the Universal Declaration of Human Rights, which was drafted by a Canadian. In 1956 we brokered the deal to end the Suez Crisis, for which Mr. Pearson won the Nobel Peace Prize the next year. We did this with a core of superb, elegant and intelligent diplomats which, in 1959, a rising senator from Massachusetts named John F. Kennedy called "perhaps the finest in the world."

All this we did and more. Together, arms, alms, ideas and envoys gave us presence in the world. We found the money, we found the energy, and we found the imagination because we thought we should do it. I cannot say that we did it with a great sense of mission, or as "an idea of Canada". But clearly there was something of that in the address that Louis St. Laurent made at the University of Toronto in 1948, when he argued that as Canada had played a seminal role in war, it must now play a seminal role in peace.

And we did just that. The world was smaller, of course, and we were comparatively larger. There was that awful shadow of war and the Cold War. Our values were different then but so were our ambitions. I would say that we had ambitions then, however undeclared they may have been. There were no white papers or foreign policy statements -- just a sense of what was possible, what was necessary and what was right, and a leadership that understood that. In other words, we had an idea of ourselves in the world. It was uncloaked in rhetoric but it was, nonetheless, an idea.

Somehow we got away from that a generation or more ago. We went to sleep. We built a generous social welfare state and argued over Quebec and national unity, which is what we wanted to do or what we had to do. By the middle of the 1960s, bearing the burden of our internationalism became too heavy and we let our diplomacy, our defence and our developmental assistance wither. Our commitment to foreign aid as a percentage of our national wealth never did reach 0.7 percent. In fact it reached its peak of 0.53 percent in 1975-76. By the 2002, in terms of aid, we had fallen to 19th place among the top 22 donor nations of the OECD. Money aside, we were in too many countries. We disbursed aid to some 150 countries, and we were in too many sectors with too few resources.

Our diplomacy, as well, had become unfocussed in the middle of the 1990s. True, we helped to push through the treaties banning anti-personnel landmines and establishing of the International Criminal Court. But I think we overstated the importance of both, given that many influential nations did not sign them. Meanwhile, smaller countries like Norway were doing the heavy lifting in international affairs. (I refer to the Oslo process in the Middle East.) Meanwhile our proud foreign service was becoming a shadow of its former self, suffering from problems of recruitment and retention and becoming the lowest-paid profession among all government departments. Diplomacy was no longer a priesthood or a calling; it was a stepping stone to the private sector or consulting for so many people.

And lastly of the three Ds, there was the military. You people know all about that, of course, but just ask yourself: what does it say about a country in which a leading military historian can write a best-selling book called *Who Killed the Canadian Military?*

Andrew Cohen

I do not say that this decline, this disinvestment, this disarmament was conscious. In fact it was probably unconscious. We never discussed it. There was no national debate, no tearing of hair, no renting of clothes. No Minister of the Crown ever got up and announced: "We are going to withdraw from the world and we are going to do that by under-funding the arms of our internationalism." It was not that clear, but austerity and apathy conspired to bring us to where we are today, and we have accepted a culture of decline even as we still think that we were as generous a donor, as effective a peacekeeper and warrior, and as a skilled a diplomat as we were in decades past. That has been the collective impact of our decisions. Our decline is not the product of one political party, one period, one policy, or one person. It is just the accumulated weight of so many internal concerns -- a blissful unawareness of the parochial, insular Canada that we were creating. It was a Canada breaking faith with its history, its geography, its prosperity and its diversity. It was becoming what I call a 'Potemkin Canada' -- a kind of colourful facade, a Canada which liked to think that it was still doing great things in the world when in fact it was not.

That is the argument of decline, of Canada having fallen asleep. It is one I've been making over the last three or four years. Still, things have changed a little bit recently, and I would suggest that there is good news. The good news is that this argument, the "declinist" argument, has largely been accepted by the government, however grudgingly and haltingly. Declinists find some support in a recent study called *External Voices* by Robert Greenhill, who is now the President of CIDA. Published by the Canadian Institute of International Affairs, it surveys 40 or so prominent foreigners who by and large subscribe to the declinist school of thought. The fact that foreigners are telling us this has had, I think, a little more impact in Canada.

It is also the language of the new foreign policy statement which talks about reclaiming Canada's role in the world and laments what happened to our capabilities. So, if you believe that the acknowledgement of ignorance is the beginning of wisdom, this is progress. A change of leadership in Ottawa has made a difference here. I think Prime Minister Paul Martin is comfortable in the world in a way his predecessor was not. Martin is the son of a foreign minister and he's been engaged in the world for a long time. He revels in policy. When he came to office he said he would make foreign policy one of his top three priorities. (Admittedly, those were the days when he had only three priorities, but I think he has made it a priority).

Since December of 2003 the progress has been fitful, but there is a pattern here, and it is one generally of trying to return Canada to the world. In other words, after 10 years or more of drift and dissembling there is something happening here. If we aren't fully awake yet, at least we're stirring.

And why do I say that? Largely because a few things have materially changed over the last 18 months. Some are more broadly thematic. The prime minister is pushing (I do not know with what amount of success) an idea of the leaders of 20 leading countries (L-20) meeting to discuss global challenges. This was Paul Martin's idea. The L-20 is meant to act where the United Nations cannot. More pointedly, Martin believes in *The Responsibility to Protect*, a study of humanitarian intervention in failed or failing states. Although it was former foreign minister Lloyd Axworthy's brainchild, Martin has revived it as a blueprint for armed intervention to protect vulnerable populations from state repression or neglect. It has attracted serious comment at the United Nations and if you listen to our people in New York, it is entering the international discourse. The Prime Minster believes in UN reform - especially the re-structuring of the Security Council - and we are not alone in that.

These are ideas to which he has personally committed himself. Others are a little more concrete, but they are still taking shape. For example, the Canada Corps, which has appeared during Mr. Martin's tenure, would send some 5,000 Canadians abroad to work on democracy, nationbuilding, and development projects. The government has supported the elections in the Ukraine in 2004 by sending 500 Canadians to help monitor the polls. Their contribution was all but unnoticed because of the Asian Tsunami which happened around the same time. The effort cost us a lot of money, but it went largely unnoticed. At the same time we have supported the elections in Palestine and Iraq.

I think it is important to say that the International Policy Statement (IPS) is a serious undertaking. It is a pragmatic, focused document offering for the first time a comprehensive, integrated view of all the arms of foreign policy: defence, diplomacy, aid and trade. It talks about values - too much so in my view. But there is also talk of interests. It uses strong language, like "earning our way" and "making hard choices", like rhetoric matching resources and making a difference and being relevant, effective and timely. This is the language of progress. You would not have heard that language three or four years ago because you could find lots of people in government who would tell you about all the great things that we were doing. And once again, the IPS gingerly accepts the declinist argument and seeks to address it by assessing the roles played by the three D's.

These proceedings will focus on defence, but let's look briefly at the other two D's. Our diplomacy will henceforth be more focused, especially with regard to the United States. We may venture out into the world but we live in North America They are our neighbour and ally and we can already see a different strategy at work in Washington. It largely has a lot to do with the appointment of Frank McKenna as our ambassador. He is doing the hard, effective work that has not been done in Washington. He represents Canada not with our usual reticence and reserve, but with American moxie. That means selling Canada to the media there, whether it is writing editorials in the newspapers and going on CNN to do battle with the critics of "Soviet Canuckistan", as we are called in conservative circles.

At the same time we have also increased our diplomatic representation in the United States. We have opened new consulates and offices and we have made the United States a priority with an understanding that it is and remains our neighbour and our largest trading partner.

The ills of the diplomats themselves are being addressed, however tentatively. The department was reorganized in January and is now called Foreign Affairs Canada (FAC). This is not the kind of thing that makes headlines but it is part of a regime of reform. It has been re-oriented thematically rather than geographically to make it more responsive and efficient. The government has found money to pay our diplomats better, and they are hoping that the rates of retention and recruitment will rise. We are also investing heavily in public diplomacy. A former high-ranking foreign service officer, Paul Heinbecker, remarked that when we do something we are hopeless at selling it to a wider audience. He said that when it comes to selling an idea we are right up there with Outer Mongolia. We are trying to do a better job.

As far as aid is concerned, there is also a promise of change. The government is increasing aid at 8 percent a year, and has reduced the number of recipients from 150 countries to 25. We will target our aid to increase its impact - something that effective donors do. I would suggest to you the chapter on aid in the IPS provides some innovative thinking of what the CIDA should do and how it should do it. Recently, the government has appointed an outsider, Robert Greenhill (the same Robert Greenhill that produced *External Voices*), who is not part of the bureaucracy as the president of CIDA. He is there to shake things up. He is an agent of change supported by the Minister for International Co-operation, Aileen Carroll, whose tenure will depend on the degree to which the government will allow real imagination to flourish within the portfolio.

Once again, much of this is happening below the radar. But things are indeed happening. I would argue that what the government is attempting to do in international assistance may hold the greatest chance of success among the three D's. In aid and diplomacy we should acknowledge an energy and ambition that we have not seen in a decade or more. As well as something more important that has not been there - money. I am not going to get into the military side of things other than to say that Ottawa is going to be talking about it. What the government calls the largest financial investment in 20 years and the appointment of no-nonsense General Hillier as Chief of Defence Staff are highly positive developments. But much of this is the soft rhetoric of good intentions. The billions of dollars needed to re-build our defence may yet be held up.

When I think of where Canada is in the world and when I think of where the International Policy Statement is bringing us and what its prospects are, I think of the late Chinese Premier Zhou Enlai who, when asked to comment on the progress of the French Revolution 200 years later, said: "It's too early to say." Thus, for all we have said, for all that Mr. Martin appears to be doing in fits and starts with the IPS, I think he is yet to articulate a vision of Canada abroad. And I am not convinced that the money will be there for all that we have to do - especially re-building the military.

*The Responsibility to Protect*, for example, will be no more than an exercise in high-blown rhetoric if we do not have the resources to be a part of it. It is the same thing in aid. It was a surprise to me that this government has refused to commit Canada to reach 0.7 percent of GDP in international assistance. Britain, Germany and France, as well as Scandinavia, have already reached that level or have committed themselves to reaching it. Canada has said that we will not do that, we do not have the money, even as we approach a trillion-dollar economy. For me it is a moral failure.

Certainly there will be more aid money than there was. I think there will probably be enough to satisfy Canadians, to make them feel good about the kinds of things we are doing in the world, or that which they think we are doing, even if we are not. Moreover, in the absence of a parliamentary majority it is unlikely that the government will stick to its plans.

The good news, however, about our minority government is that the opposition parties generally support the larger themes of Canadian foreign policy. They support more money for aid, a muscular and focused diplomacy, support for the United Nations and other international institutions, support for peacekeeping and revitalising the military, and a global foreign policy rooted in North America.

There is general approval in Canada for what the government is doing. I believe Canadians think we should be in Afghanistan, and so do the other political parties. There is no one of consequence saying we should not be doing this, which is noteworthy in a country of this size. Each of the four parties generally agrees with the thrust of what we are doing abroad. The danger, of course, is finding the money, and if it begins to run out, rest assured that the first to be hit will be the arms of internationalism.

So where does that leave us? Do we now have an inspired vision of Canada in the world? Does the IPS add up to that? I would say not yet. There is not much poetry from this government and not much sense of history in this document.

# MAKING INTER-DEPARTMENTAL 'JOINTNESS' (3-D) WORK

## Mark Sedra

### Introduction

The new International Policy Statement (IPS) charts a new course for Canada's foreign and defence policy. Underlying this new approach is the recognition that today's multi-dimensional foreign policy challenges demand more sophisticated cross-governmental responses. It reflects a growing trend in Ottawa - one that aims to achieve greater cohesion and coherence in the design and implementation of policy, and thus circumvent existing departmental "silos". As such, the IPS is representative of a wider policy trend that can be detected in a number of Western countries (notably Britain and Australia) to forge whole-of-government or joined-up government policy-making processes. 3-D is the Canadian manifestation of this trend. The first attempts at fielding this approach, in Haiti and Afghanistan, have achieved some remarkable success, but also revealed its limitations within current government structures.

In an attempt to better understand this new approach, I will consider it on three levels. The first will seek to deconstruct the concept of joined-up government by asking what it really means in practice. The second will examine the application of the 3-D model in Canada, assessing its impact on decision-making. Finally, I will identify the prevailing challenges to the institutionalization of a joined-up policy-making framework and offer recommendations on how they can be overcome.

### Deconstructing the Concept

In defining joined-up government and its Canadian corollary, 3-D, it is important

---

**Mark Sedra** is a Cadieux-Léger Fellow at Foreign Affairs Canada. The views expressed by Mr. Sedra do not necessarily reflect the position of Foreign Affairs Canada.

to clarify the distinction between the two related concepts. The notion of joined-up government, popularized in the United Kingdom, has a wider scope than 3-D, implying a genuinely whole-of-government orientation. 3-D, by contrast, can be defined in a more limited manner as encompassing the three agencies at the forefront of Canadian international policy: diplomacy (through Foreign Affairs Canada); defence (through the Department of National Defence), and development (through the Canadian International Development Agency). However, both approaches are premised on the recognition that many of the most pressing issues facing governments today are cross-cutting in nature, and accordingly require multi-departmental solutions. As they share the same conceptual underpinnings, the two approaches will often be used interchangeably in this presentation.

The Australian Public Service Commission describes the concept as follows:

> [Joined-up government] denotes public service agencies working across portfolio boundaries to achieve a shared goal and an integrated government response to particular issues. [These approaches] can be formal and informal. They can focus on policy development, program or service delivery.

The concept is intended to foster horizontal decision-making and action, circumventing the proclivity for vertical management, often referred to as departmentalism. The goal is to overcome the "silos" created by departmentalism and vertical styles of management, and to balance inclusion in public policy development with the unwelcome effect of "many hands in the pie".

Joined-up government is not a panacea, nor is it appropriate in all circumstances. The costs and benefits of adopting a cross-cutting approach, rather than relying on more traditional modes of decision-making are illustrated below and must be weighed carefully.

**Joined-up Government: A Cost-Benefit Analysis**

| Benefits | Costs |
|---|---|
| • Permits the development of more sophisticated and nuanced analyses of multi-disciplinary issues. | • Less visible lines of accountability and responsibility for policy and service delivery. |
| • Addresses transcendent cross-cutting issues not covered by the mandates of any individual department. | • Greater difficulty in measuring effectiveness and impact, due to the need to develop new and more sophisticated performance measurement systems. |

| Benefits | Costs |
|---|---|
| • Supports the development of cross-departmental synergies that maximize the effectiveness of policy and, or, service delivery. | • Direct and opportunity costs of management and staff time spent establishing and sustaining cross-citing working arrangements. |
| • Facilitates cross-departmental resource mobilization. | • The multiplicity of actors involved in policy-making process can slow decision-making. |
| • Exploits economies of scale through sharing of Information Technology (IT) facilities, data, and other assets. | • Can weaken organizational loyalty and cohesion. |
| • Provides a framework to resolve inter-agency disputes and make trade-offs. | |

Joined-up government is a necessary evolution in the policy-making field that has paralleled fundamental changes in the international security environment. The threat of inter-state conventional war has receded, replaced by an array of transnational security threats such as terrorism, international crime, environmental degradation, state failure, disease, poverty, and internal conflict. This has stimulated a new understanding of "human security", emphasizing the security of individuals rather than regimes.

These new types of security concerns are too complex to be addressed through departmental "silos"; they necessitate multi-dimensional approaches that break down the boundaries separating development, diplomacy, and defence. For instance, in a failed state one cannot advance development or foster good governance and institutional renewal without security, often provided by international forces. Similarly, long-term peace and security cannot be assured without sustainable development, advanced by development agencies, and good governance or peace processes, supported by diplomatic missions. To succeed in this environment, government agencies must adapt their policies to reflect the fluid and interconnected nature of contemporary threats and crises.

**The Canadian Model of Joined-up Government: 3-D**

As mentioned previously, 3-D is a uniquely Canadian adaptation of the joined-up government model, designed to advance Canada's international policy objectives. Such approaches have yet to be replicated in the domestic policy arena. Prime Minister Paul Martin described the 3-D approach during his visit to Washington, DC on 29 April, 2004:

In Canada, we refer to the three D's - defence, diplomacy and development. This means we are integrating our traditional foreign policy instruments more tightly, especially when responding to the need of vulnerable states to build up their own capacity to govern themselves. As Afghanistan has demonstrated, even the presence of foreign troops cannot guarantee security unless there is also progress towards a political settlement. But, equally, there will be no political settlement unless security is established. And proper economic development needs both - security and political stability - if it is to work.

The main thrust of the 3-D agenda is to enhance Canada's capacity to engage fragile and failed states. In this regard, Canadian operations in Haiti and Afghanistan have become critical test cases of the concept.

*Haiti*

All three "Ds" are well represented in the Haitian context. The defence component was represented by a Canadian contribution to the Interim Multinational Force and the deployment of 100 police officers to the Mission des Nations-Unies pour la Stabilisation d'Haiti (MINUSTAH). In terms of diplomacy, diplomats contributed to important resolutions on Haiti at the Organization of American States, the UN, and CARICOM. Finally, on the development side, Canada led donor discussions on the Interim Cooperation Framework, which outlines a four-pronged strategy for short- to medium-term reconstruction. Canada also pledged to support the resulting Interim Cooperation Framework with contributions of $45 million in each of the next two years.

*Afghanistan*

More so than Haiti, Afghanistan has become the "poster child" for the 3-D approach. The complexity of the Afghan case has provided a demanding testing ground for the concept. In Afghanistan, the process has largely been Kabul-driven; Canadian actors on the ground have been able to promote the 3-D agenda effectively without having to refer all decisions back to their respective ministerial headquarters in Ottawa.

In terms of defence, Canada was one of the largest contributors to the NATO-led International Security Assistance Force (ISAF) established in 2002. Its more recent deployment of a 250-person Provincial Reconstruction Team (PRT) to the southern city of Kandahar will be backed up by 1,000 extra troops when Canada assumes control of the Southern Regional Command in early 2006. On the diplomatic front, Canada played a key role in the Bonn political process and provided indispensable support to the parliamentary and presidential elections. In terms of development, demilitarization and landmine action have benefited from CIDA's support, and Ottawa has committed over $600-million of aid through 2009, making Afghanistan the single largest recipient of Canadian bilateral aid.

The robust nature of the defence and development pillars buttressed the diplomatic arm immensely. They have raised Canada's prestige and influence, giving Canadian officials a seat at every important decision-making table in Kabul. This imbued the Canadian embassy with tremendous leverage with which to pursue Canadian interests. However, the development and defence pillars did not seek to leverage diplomatic assets in comparable fashion, representing a missed opportunity. The ability to identify such opportunities and capitalize on them highlights one area in need of improvement.

**The Provincial Reconstruction Team (PRT)**

One popular application of the 3-D approach that has emerged in Afghanistan is the Provincial Reconstruction Team. Currently there are 21 PRTs operating throughout Afghanistan. Canada assumed command of the Kandahar PRT in August of 2005. The importance of the PRT has transcended Afghanistan; it has become a model that will likely be imitated in other post-conflict settings.

The PRTs, and the activities of all three "Ds" encapsulated within them, are structured around four comprehensive goals:

1. Assist in the development of a legitimate Afghan security and political infrastructure by building Afghan institutional capacity and supporting the legitimate Afghan government.

2. Facilitate reconstruction by initiating and prioritizing reconstruction projects, promoting economic development and coordinating with UN agencies, NGOs and Afghan government officials.

3. Develop close working relationships with Afghan government ministries, UN agencies and NGOs at the provincial level in order to promote unity of effort in achieving common objectives.

4. Enhance security by developing relationships with the local population, promoting knowledge of on-going international and Afghan government efforts, collecting and disseminating intelligence and defeating anti-government insurgents, warlords and other "spoiler" groups.

The Canadian PRT focuses on security sector reform and governance, and consists of roughly 250 Canadian Forces personnel, two Foreign Affairs Canada officials, one representative from CIDA, and 1-2 representatives from the RCMP. There are a number of potential points of tension within the Canadian PRT, common among many other NATO- and Coalition-led PRTs deployed across the country, that are rooted in the 3-D model. These include:

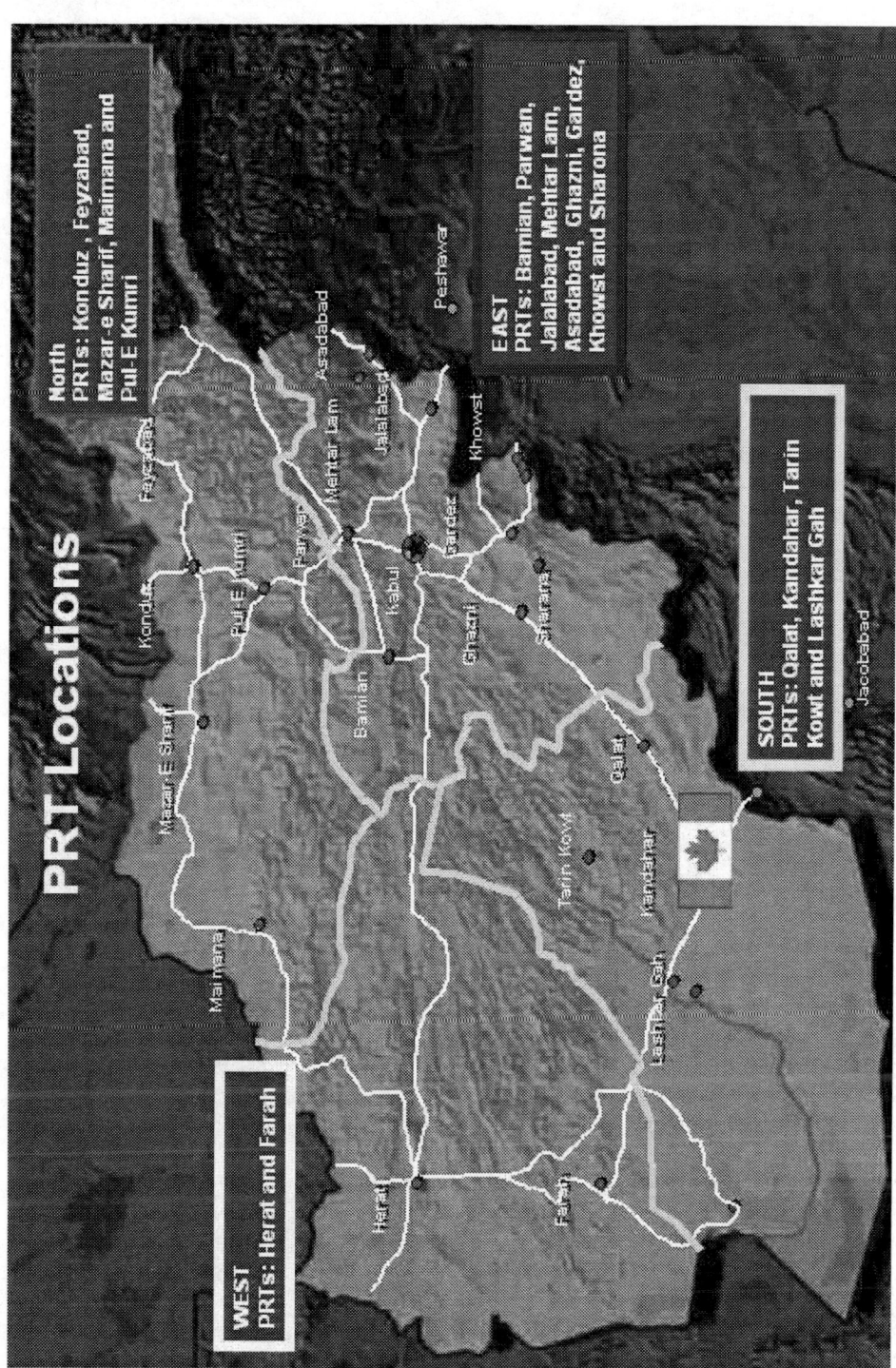

- To whom do the civilian representatives report?

- What measures of effectiveness have been established for the civilian component?

- Who will be the principal point of contact on civilian issues?

This suggests that certain areas of the 3-D approach require further elaboration and refinement. The PRTs are a viable representation of the 3-D approach in the field, but for them to be successful they must be supported by appropriate government architecture in Ottawa.

## Government Architecture

The elements of an emergent 3-D architecture are being developed in Ottawa, and have found expression in the nascent Stabilization and Reconstruction Task Force (START) and the Global Peace and Security Fund (GPSF). START is a formal standing body intended to facilitate rapid joined-up government responses to international crises. The GPSF is a commitment of $100-million annually over the next five years to "support urgent contributions to crisis response operations, as well as measures to ensure lasting human security." These are the first of the formal and permanent mechanisms needed to establish continuity in the 3-D approach. Traditionally, 3-D has been manifested in the formation of Task Forces to confront crises as they arise, such as the current Sudan Task Force. This approach is not conducive to building institutional memory, better served by the formation of standing bodies. One of START's key functions is knowledge management, to make sure that the lessons of past interventions are absorbed. Cumulatively, these two bodies will ensure that Canada's responses to crises are no longer reactive and *ad hoc* in nature.

To date, the different departments have viewed the 3-D concept in different ways. For DND, the experience in the Balkans and Afghanistan illustrated that progress in state-building is the key to their exit strategy. Creating conditions conducive for the military's disengagement is dependent on the effective delivery of development assistance by CIDA and the advancement of governance reform and reconciliation processes by Foreign Affairs. As such, they have adopted the notion out of necessity.

Foreign Affairs champions the concept because they see themselves as the natural leader of it. They see it as a means to extend a degree of control over the activities of other government departments. Mechanisms like START show that FAC recognizes the need for a broad consultative process, as long as it articulates its own policy goals.

CIDA has been the most reluctant to embrace the concept, which it views with suspicion. In particular, it is organically wary of military solutions. Some at CIDA see 3-D as an attempt to subordinate legitimate long-term development objectives to short-term military imperatives. As well, there has always been antagonism between CIDA and Foreign Affairs, because CIDA possesses the project funding while Foreign Affairs has the policy lead.

**Assessing Canada's Record**

3-D is very situational and issue-specific. On some issues it works extremely well; on others, less so. Every issue demands the engagement of a different constellation of actors from across government. Often the level of integration and cohesion achieved is dictated by the personality of the actors involved. The departments may disagree on individual issues, but are characteristically unanimous on the utility of consultation. Hence, they agree to disagree.

One 3-D success story within the government architecture is the setting of Guidelines on Humanitarian Action and Civil-Military Coordination. They took two years to develop and represent a seminal accomplishment. Other notable successes are the negotiation of Standard Operating Procedures on Disaster Relief, the heavy weapons cantonment program in Afghanistan, and the formation and operation of the Disaster Assistance Response Team (DART).

But alongside these successes are vexing problems. The IPS clearly demonstrates the difficulties in realizing the 3-D vision by virtue of the fact the former was released in four separate books. The IPS is not indicative of unified and seamless government policy. It is an amalgamation of three separate policies that reflects three independent agendas. It represents a bureaucratic refusal to understand the perspectives and agendas of other departments. Each department still features unique doctrinal and disciplinary approaches, internal dynamics, and methods of operation. Put simply, they still view the same issues differently. The process of arriving at the IPS is indicative of the extent to which 3-D has percolated down through the bureaucracy.

Process and decision-making follow structure. As long as existing structures remain unchanged, the various federal departments will continue to advance their own interests, protecting their mandates and resources. As long as structures remain static, joined-up government will, in practice, be nothing more than intensive consultations. Is this qualitatively different from the period before the emergence of the joined-up government notion? Some argue that 3-D is merely a new term to describe what was already occurring, an attempt to re-package and re-brand existing practices. In the face of such criticism and scepticism it is important to remain cognizant that integrating government decision-making is a long-term process. We are, after all, working against generations of entrenched institutional culture.

## Challenges and the road ahead

Undoubtedly, there are several obstacles to the successful implementation of a joined-up government approach in Canada. Among the most prominent are:

- Insufficient common analysis and information sharing. Analysis is not always shared, nor are policy and programming prescriptions.

- Poor assessments of past interventions and practices. We are not learning the institutional lessons.

- Vertical management and reporting lines. Departments sometimes have a tendency to wait for an internal consensus to be reached prior to engaging their counterparts in other government departments. This can cause damaging delays.

- Turf wars, mistrust, stereotypes, and perennial fears (i.e. FAC is after funding, the military cannot contribute to political or development issues, or that CIDA's purview is programming and not policy) have yet to be overcome.

- Lack of transparency. Often internal decision-making processes on cross-cutting issues are not shared with other engaged departments, creating confusion.

- Focus on short-term departmental objectives rather than corporate whole-of-government goals. In preparing common policies, the individual departments often appear more concerned with ensuring their own interests are met rather than developing a coherent national policy.

- Problems of funding and accountability. Our bureaucratic structures do not yet allow for maximal leveraging of resources to facilitate timely decisions and enhance policy impacts.

- Lack of a common language, integrated IT systems and classifications. Sometimes technology is not compatible, causing costly delays in the dissemination of information.

- Problems of rotationality. The adverse effects of rotationality must be recognized and mechanisms built in to ensure continuity. For example, FAC and CIDA personnel are often confined to 1-year rotations while military personnel adhere to 6-month tours.

In order overcome these obstacles, steps will need to be taken that go beyond the foundation set by the IPS. These would include:

- Establishing new performance indicators that emphasize cross-cutting objectives. Inject 3-D into employment profiles and terms of reference.

- More interchange of staff between departments. Cross-fertilisation is critical. Joint training provides one means to advance this goal.

- Ministers and senior civil servants should become "champions" of inter-departmental integration and cross-sectoral policies. The concept must be more aggressively pushed down the bureaucratic chain.

- Adjust accountability structures to reflect the need for inter-departmental connectivity. A change in emphasis in accountability away from solely quantitative measures of inputs and outputs toward more qualitative evaluations of performance is needed.

- More flexibility in the funding of cross-cutting policies, including the use of pooled funds. Further changes to budgetary rules are needed to make it easier for departments to move money between years, organizations and budgets in order to promote cross-cutting work. It is necessary to create national integrated budgets.

- Improve information and intelligence sharing, engage in joint analysis.

- Any barriers or disincentives to cross-cutting working due to audit and inspection systems should be minimised.

- Synchronize IT and classification systems.

- Reinforce Standing Inter-Ministerial Bodies (START).

- Move from 3-D to a genuine whole-of-government approach. To do so, studies must be conducted to map government capacity on specific international issues. A mechanism should be established to mobilize civil society to fill gaps in government capacity.

## Conclusion

It is clear that the growing complexity of existing foreign policy challenges, such as failed and fragile states, necessitate more sophisticated policy responses. Traditional modes of policy-making, undertaken through vertical silos, are increasingly ill-suited to respond to contemporary threats. The 3-D model represents an attempt to re-shape the policy-making landscape to reflect our increasingly inter-connected world. It aims to bridge departmental divides and foster integrated decision-making.

The first concerted Canadian application of the model, in Afghanistan, clearly demonstrated the utility of this new approach. Harmonizing Canada's defence, diplomacy, and development activities greatly enhanced Canada's influence in the country. This is not to say that the Afghan 3-D experiment was without its problems. Tellingly, the breakdowns in the process that did occur happened at the headquarters level in Ottawa, not in the field. It illustrated the challenge of overcoming the doctrinal divisions between the departments, which were particularly acute on issues such as civil-military relations.

Is it possible to move beyond 3-D? Can we establish a genuinely whole-of-government approach capable of mobilizing resources and expertise across the wide breadth of government to advance Canada's interests internationally? Nascent structures such as START and the GPSF represent important initial steps toward this goal, but much more has to be done.

In many ways we have reached a threshold in our efforts to institutionalize the joined-up government concept. Overcoming this threshold in order to make horizontal decision-making the norm demands more than just the establishment of new structures. It requires a change of mindsets and systemic institutional reforms. Above all, it requires the modernization of ingrained institutional cultures. While important steps have been made to achieve greater cohesion in the formulation of Canada's international policy, achieving a genuinely whole-of-government framework is still many years away.

# THE NEW DEFENCE AGENDA

## Dr. Douglas Bland

I would like to talk about what we call the new defence agenda, but let me first put the cards on the table. Strategic studies and strategic studies research results do not matter greatly in the formulation and continuation of defence policy. If we get that message wrong, if you do not understand how Canadian defence policy is actually made, we are going to miss the policy world and become irrelevant.

Some might argue that many of the great academic works of the strategic studies community have, since the 1990s, set the stage for the present defence policy statement and the increase in funding for the Canadian Forces. If we are to believe that we will have to review those policy documents to find references to any of those studies. Such references are not there. I cannot find any quotes. For instance, are there many Canadian strategic studies papers in the last 10 years that suggested a significant increase in funding for the Canadian Forces could be delayed for five more years? I will concede that some, but not many, of the papers and commentary produced by academe and by organizations such as the CISS and Conference of Defence Associations (CDA) contributed to a degree of public worry about the Canadian Forces, if not about national defence policy in general. But public concern was also generated by news coverage of conditions faced by soldiers in the field, and the difficulties they encountered while on operations.

But what moved the Liberal party off its default position of putting national defence on the back burner? Strategic studies or burning submarines? What I argue, and it is not new, is that the Canadian government's position changed because it was faced with a political liability. It is the political liability they are responding to, and they are trying to snuff it out. And they are doing rather well. They have given the

---

**Dr. Douglas Bland** is Chair of Defence Management Studies, Queen's University.

Dr. Douglas Bland

Chief of Defence Staff, a friend of mine and a sincere man, a free hand to take corrective measures within the Canadian Forces as he sees fit. They have also made a promise of money some time in the future.

(Just as an aside, Andrew Cohen mentioned that the key word in the Liberal message is that this is the greatest advance in defence spending in 20 years. Actually, 24 years ago Pierre Trudeau was in power, and he only started spending on national defence after irrefutable evidence of a commitment-capabilities gap emerged, and allegations of the rust-out of the armed forces and broken down machinery all over Europe were too numerous to ignore. When Brian Mulroney and the Conservative party started beating on him about Canada without armed forces, Trudeau boosted spending. That was 20 years ago.)

Thus when you have a political liability in Canada, the thing to do is throw money at it. So what drives the defence policy beyond the rhetoric of occasional White Papers? Defence Minister Brooke Claxton warned senior military officers in 1951 about strategic planning regarding NATO. He warned them that what they were offering the government was unrealistic and ignored the facts of national life, upon which policy must be built. Robert Sutherland, a defence scientist in 1963 advised Defence Minister Paul Hellyer that a wholly Canadian strategic rational for defence "does not exist and cannot be invented". Nevertheless, Hellyer attempted to invent a Canadian strategy but Prime Minister Lester Pearson dismissed it out of hand, saying that Canada did not need an efficient armed force.

In the defence paper of the 1970s, Trudeau's government declared that "it is not possible simply to state defence requirements and call that the defence budget." He went on to say rather that "defence decisions including budgetary decisions ought to be based on the judgment and selection of activities in relation to other government operations."

In 1994 the new Liberal government spent months researching defence policy options, and encouraged a joint committee of the Senate and House of Commons to conduct a wide-ranging view of defence policy - a review which engaged nearly every leading scholar of strategic studies in Canada. Ottawa ultimately dismissed the committee's detailed report as "inconsistent with the financial parameters within which the Department of National Defence must operate." It is the facts of national life that drive defence policy in Canada, and these facts are based in domestic political attitudes and domestic political needs, not from any assessment of the global strategic picture. Besides, Canada's defence policy is not that complicated. How many studies do we need to tell us that there is no threat, and if there was one, the Americans will save us? How many times do we have to listen to Joel Sokolsky from the Royal Military College of Canada tell us that Canada's defence problem is that Canada has no defence problem. I would even quote Senator Raoul Durandan. When he was asked once what should Canada's foreign defence policies be, his answer was "Be quiet and give no cause for alarm." Sounds like the Iraq policy in 2003. But how many times do we have to explain that Canada has two strategic imperatives: defend Canada and defend North American in co-operation with the United States. From one strategic choice, everything else follows. These are enduring strategic messages that do not change much over time.

The objectives of Canadian defence policy, which cannot be disassociated from foreign policy, are: to preserve the peace by supporting collective defence measures; to deter military aggression; to support Canadian foreign policy, including that arising out of our participation in international organizations, and; to provide for the protection and surveillance of our territory, our airspace and costal waters. This was true in Paul Hellyer's time - 1964 to be precise. It seems good enough today. The agenda of the 1990s and before was to make strategic studies arguments - some sophisticated, some rather problematic, some simply self-serving and devoid of respect for the enduring facts of national life.

If you wish to believe that the Prime Minister was jolted into action by the brilliant strategic studies papers from, say, Queen's University, and that this caused him to rally his cabinet, get the keys to the treasury, give them to the CDS, and tell him to go take all he wants, you are free to do so. Strategic studies attempts to reveal a rational for what needs to be done for national defence with the hope that the government will see the light. But the only thing the government sees in national defence policy is, as General Guy Simmons would have said if he were here, that defence policy is expensive and unpopular.

Since 1952, no government In Canada has provided to national defence what was needed. Governments provide what is available for national defence, not what is needed for national defence. Again, to paraphrase Joel Sokolsky, the government provides how much for national defence? Just enough to get by. The reality is the government says to the defence minister, in modern times, here is $13-billion. Go see what you can do with that, and do not come back. Actual defence policy outcomes, capabilities and so on are determined not by strategic studies, but by the defence budget and how policies are administered. The new defence agenda is aimed at highlighting this distinction in order to get the most performance out of the resources DND is given.

Let me digress for a minute. What is the purpose of armed forces? Their purpose is to provide coercive force (or the threat of coercive force) to be used at the discretion of the government. The aim of defence policy is to describe the where, when, how and with whom you will use that coercive force. The aim of defence administration is to organize, equip, sustain and hold ready the coercive forces. Efficiencies of defence administration must be measured against these objectives. Put simply, how well does the system produce combat output? The amount of money any government is going to provide for national defence over the next number of years can be predicted with some confidence. The floor is 1% of GDP and is established by the squeals of our allies and organizations such as the CISS and the CDA. The ceiling is 2% of GDP, established by the squeals of the finance minister and the political left in Canada. That is essentially the background.

We know what we want the armed forces to do, we know what the funding levels are going to be, we know that to increase Canada's defence potential, the way to do it is to ruthlessly manage the "just enough" that the government gives the armed forces to carry out its policies. So let us look at how we do that.

In 1947, General Charles Foulkes set the standard for National Defence Headquarters. It ought to be, he said, a small, thinking headquarters, devoid of administrative responsibility. We are not there yet, and in fact the reality may be the complete opposite. The latest study commissioned by former Defence Minister John McCallum, called the *Minister's Efficiency Study*, has a ring of truth to it, and a good feel for the general state of the problem. The report states there are many things done at Headquarters that do not need to be done there, or anywhere else for that matter.

The new defence agenda poses questions about what needs to be done and how do we do it efficiently, where combat output is the measure of success. Again, the main theme of the new agenda is that the purpose of the Canadian Forces is to act as an instrument of controlled coercion. The question that we want to ask is not what do we want the Canadian Forces to do, but at what level of intensity, efficiency and scope do we want the Canadian Forces to do the principal things that armed forces do, and then apply that to various situations. We always have these questions about what we want the armed forces to do, and once we settle that, well everything else will fall into place. Nobody ever asks that about police forces. Have you ever seen a White Paper about policing in Toronto in which the citizens ask what they would like the police to do? But we seem to ask that question of the armed forces. Clearly we are mixing up the question of what we would like armed (the word is important) forces to do with the question of whether they should be armed or not.

Let me touch on a few of the items in the new defence agenda. Again, from the *Minister's Efficiency Study*, one of the first things to do is to recognize that national defence is a national effort of the government; it is not a public good produced solely by the Department of National Defence. National defence is not the responsibility of the Canadian Forces; they are merely an instrument of policy. National defence is the responsibility of the whole of government. That means all the departments. And that is evident in all our policies.

The second thing is to decide what we mean in terms of dollars, capabilities and so on for coercive force? How much, what scale, scope and so on. We need to look at that and how to produce it. We need to know who is doing what and how does what they are doing contribute or not contribute to producing combat output.

We need to talk about defence procurement, and people are beginning to do so. Mark Sedra spoke about "joined-up government". Defence procurement in Canada is like joined-up government, or rather jammed-up government. For example, a Major Crown Project - anything that costs more than $100-million - involves at least nine departments and agencies of government and people outside government. If it is a smaller project, more people get involved. Try convening a meeting of nine department heads in Ottawa anytime soon. We need to look at how we produce combat output more rationally and quickly.

We need to adopt a bias in favour of combatants. Of the more or less 60,000 people in the CF, how many of those are front line, at the sharp end of the spear, and how many are at the blunt end? Why do we have more than 80 classifications for officers and non-commissioned members? I know that talking about the old days is not always good, but in the 1960s, everyone in the army (and there were more than 50,000 of them) was grouped into only 11 classifications and that included nurses, doctors, dentists and so on. Why do we have all these branches of the service with all their own managers? We need to talk about active re-allocation. By that I mean taking things from the blunt end of the spear and putting them in the sharp end of the spear.

The main message for joined-up government regarding the new policy issues that are not mentioned in the new policy statement comes from the *Minister's Efficiency Study*: "Without fundamental transformation of the national level of management framework and practice of the government, the Department of National Defence, the CF will not be able to transform itself rapidly enough to adapt to Canada's strategic environment."

To conclude, some might think that I began on a pessimistic note. Cheer up, because it is going to get worse. Two years ago some of us began a project with a Toronto-based organization - Breakout Educational Network - the people who produced the award-winning series *A Question of Honour*. We called the new project the "seven-year project". The term comes from the time, we felt back then, that it would take to transform, and rebuild the CF with significant, government-wide interest in doing so. The time line is very close because, as some of us argued in the pamphlet, *Canada Without Armed Forces*, we only had seven years (maybe less) before significant capabilities fell apart. It is now year five. Even with the full support of the government, the transformation is going to be difficult, if not impossible, before we run into great difficulties.

We could do better if we wanted. In 1950, the Canadian military had about 30,000 people with propeller-driven airplanes, old ships and broken-down bases. (I know. I lived on one.) By 1956-57, it boasted 120,000 people with new bases across the country, membership in NORAD, the construction of the Pine Tree Line and Mid-Canada Lines, a superb jet-driven air force, 10,000 people in the army deployed to Europe and 12 air force squadrons in Europe. A peacekeeping force had been sent to Egypt, and we had fought in the Korean War. In essence, the government of the day saw that defence under-funding hobbles our foreign policy. They came, they saw and they got to work. Today our parliament has been presented with a crisis of defence and foreign policy, and the response is they came, they saw and they ran away.

# SON OF GLOBAL MOBILE: THE HISTORICAL ORIGINS OF THE NEW DEFENCE POLICY[1]

Dr. Sean Maloney

**Introduction**

Canada's new defence policy, unveiled in 2005, echoes strongly the concepts dating back to the early 1960s. Long forgotten, distorted over time, and reviled by many, the original intent of that 40-year-old conceptualization is relevant today.

In response to the changing global strategic environment in the 1960s, brought on by a stabilizing deterrent system and de-colonization, Canadian military planners sought out a force structure that could operate effectively across the spectrum of conflict in order to provide the government of the day with as many force options as possible so that immediate resort to nuclear weapons use would be unnecessary - particularly in what they termed 'Situations Short of War'.

The purpose of this discussion is to highlight the strategic concept and force structure changes that were in the offing in 1964-1965. It will become clear how advanced and prescient Canada was in these areas. It is also a cautionary tale, for there was no happy ending. For a variety of reasons, the far-sighted planning was never fully implemented. Indeed, one can look back and even call it the conceptual equivalent of the abandonement of the Avro Arrow fighter project.

**Canada's Strategic Position in the 1960s**

In the early 1960s North Atlantic Treaty Organization (NATO) was holding the line in Western Europe and in the North Atlantic. The North American Airspace Defence (NORAD) Command, along with Canadian and US naval forces, secured

---

**Dr. Sean Maloney** is an Associate Professor of War Studies at the Royal Military College of Canada.

North America. American and Australian forces were forward-deployed in the Pacific. The expansion of Soviet and American strategic nuclear capacities were, once the major crises over Berlin and Cuba subsided, moving towards a stable deterrent system. The battlegrounds of the Cold War shifted towards areas peripheral to the defined NATO area - namely the Middle East, Africa, Asia, Central and South America.

In 1955, Canadian strategic analysis predicted that a nuclear/conventional stand-off in Europe would produce a situation whereby the Soviets and their proxies would seek to expand their influence in these areas, and slowly draw them into the communist orbit over time. The Third World was ripe for the ideological picking; much of it was in the process of de-colonizing and searching for a new way. But de-colonization was not a smooth process, as Canada found out in the 1956 Suez Crisis and particularly in the Congo from 1960 to 1964.

Dr Sean Maloney

In 1963, a far-sighted analysis of the global situation projected out to the 1980s became a key document in what would become the 1964 White Paper on Defence. This analysis strongly influenced the thinking behind the creation of Forces Mobile Command, a joint command created in 1965 as part of the integration and unification policies of the Pearson government. Some of the salient points from the document included:

- The diffusion of political, economic, and military power to areas of the world recently subject to external domination;

- The revolution of rising expectations and the consequent threats to political stability and international order;

- The development of strident nationalism in Asia, Africa, and Latin America which represents to a significant degree a self-conscious reaction against European influences;

- The impact upon social and political institutions of applied science and technology;

- The tendency towards European unity;

- The challenge of Bolshevik ideology and Russian imperialism;

- China's prospective emergence as a world power.

This was 1963, but the authors could well have been depicting the world of 1993 or 2003, if one replaces Bolshevism with radical Islam as the dominant ideological threat. Under the section called "Black Africa", the authors noted that "it is unlikely that the economic achievements of the African countries will match their aspirations. The result will be embitterment and political instability."

Who was going to police all of this? Not the UN, for according to the authors:

> The General Assembly also seems certain to retain its present character: a debating forum which reflects neither the realities of power nor a political consensus....any substantial change in the UN must be based upon a major change in the international system. This, however, will not prevent the proliferation of ingenious schemes by persons who being unable to reform the world, believe they can reform the United Nations.

The Commonwealth was not going to either. "It seems probable that by 1990, the Commonwealth, if it exists at all, will have ceased to be a significant factor in world affairs." As for the United States, "It is a near certainty that in 1990, as in 1963, the United States will be the most powerful nation in the world."

But the authors cautioned that:

> [T]he effectiveness of US policy will be constrained by the limitation of US power and by the characteristics of the US political system including its tendency to hyper-publicity, vulnerability to organized pressure groups and periodic paralysis owing to elections or impasse between President and Congress. The United States will neither be able nor inclined to bear the burdens of mankind. The United States will have need of allies.

The authors suggested, amongst many options, that Canada might want to create a "triphibious force" that could be used in the eastern Mediterranean and north Norway to support NATO, and "might conceivably be employed in support of the UN or might be used as an instrument of Canadian foreign policy outside the NATO area." Responding to suggestions that Canada pull out of NATO and create a triphibious force and turn it over to the UN, the authors caustically pointed out that:

> Some...have argued that a triphibious force would be a means of enabling Canada to give more effective military support to the United Nations and that this is sufficient reason for acquiring such a force...This argument seems to involve three distinct fallacies. The first is that the United Nations is unlikely to sponsor small wars of the

> kind for which such a force would be required. The second fallacy is that if the United Nations were to engage in such operations and would be prepared to employ Canada as its agent. The third...is that Canada would be prepared to act as an agent of the United Nations in such an event...It is clear that the United Nations cannot wage war against a recognized government. The role of any military force deployed under UN auspices must be limited to the verification of a political agreement, establishing a UN presence, or resisting threats to internal order. If a UN force cannot enter upon its duties peacefully and with the consent of all involved, almost certainly it cannot enter upon these duties at all.

Some argued for a US Marine Corps concept, and to this the response was more positive:

> A Canadian triphibious force would represent a very significant military capability in many parts of the world such as Southeast Asia or West Africa. Canada would not possess the ability to make war on her own account. She would, however, be able to play a significant role in major military operations in these areas. If it were Canada's policy to assert a significant military presence in Southeast Asia, the Caribbean, or some similar area, there would be much to be said for the concept of a triphibious force.

## Defence Re-structuring and New Concepts

By 1964, the defence policy of the Pearson government directed the disbandment of the existing military commands and the creation of new ones. The three service headquarters disappeared and were replaced with a single Canadian Forces Headquarters. The army, navy, and air force ceased to exist and in their place a number of joint commands emerged. One of these was Forces Mobile Command (FMC). It is critical to understand that FMC was not to be "the army". It evolved into "the army" by the early 1970s, but that was not the intention.

In the 1960s, Canadian land forces had a brigade group forward-deployed in West Germany serving with NATO, while another brigade was tasked to reinforce NATO's central region. A third brigade group was tasked with NATO flank operations with Allied Command Europe's (ACE) Mobile Force (Land), while another brigade group was dedicated to North American defence. At this point there were no long-term static UN commitments that employed combat units greater than a reconnaissance squadron. The first long-term static deployment was Cyprus in 1964, which employed a battle group on a six-month rotation.

FMC, in its original conceptualization, took the three Canada-based brigade groups, added in the former Royal Canadian Air Force's (RCAF) tactical aviation assets (i.e. tactical transports) and a planned airborne regiment, all under a joint headquarters. The West Germany-based brigade would remain in place under NATO command, as would the commitment of one of the Canada-based brigade groups in the event of war. The other units mentioned would be available for other employment.

FMC planners revamped the older army ideas and produced a document called Conduct of Land Operations (CLO) in 1965. CLO was "transformational" for 1965. In addition to the familiar conventional and nuclear land battle that the army had been playing with in the 1950s, CLO recognized that there were "Situations Short of War", or scenarios ranging from a show of force, a deployment or threatened deployment of troops to a troubled area, to a fierce and prolonged battle against guerillas or insurgents.

Presciently, the FMC planners recognized that:

> [R]esponsibility to solve the problem does not rest with the military. Therefore, whatever role assigned to the armed forces it is certain to be closely linked with and will only be part of concurrent political, economic, sociological, and psychological measures. The effect of this is, firstly, that the armed forces may be called upon to participate in non-military activities, for example, soldiers may be required to restore or operate public utilities. Secondly, the tactical handling of the armed forces may be influenced to an unusual degree by the demands of other agencies; for example, the use of force...may be restricted for political, economic, or psychological reasons.

Does this not foretell the advent of today's "three-block war" scenario?

Canadian soldiers had to be wary of the fluidity of Situations Short of War:

> There will not necessarily be a readily identifiable enemy or a specific piece of territory controlled by the enemy. The hostility or friendship of warring factions may alternate from time to time. There is no ready military solution to such situations other than flexibility of mind and a clear idea of the ultimate aim to be achieved.

This sounds remarkably like modern-day Afghanistan.

It is important to understand that the authors of CLO did not differentiate, really, between peace-keeping (with the hyphen), internal security, and counter-guerilla operations. Indeed, they were describing what today is known as stabilization operations.

FMC looked at the existing force structure and connected it to a "spectrum of force employment." Both 3 Brigade and 4 Brigade were to remain mechanized so they could operate in Western Europe as part of NATO forces, however 3 Brigade would have additional responsibilities and specialization to deal with guerilla warfare. The 1 and 2 Brigades were to have a different scale of equipment and training; their roles would involve guerilla warfare, terrorism, and agitation the Situations Short of War tasks.

Each Canadian infantry brigade group (CIBG) would have a secondary role:

> 1 CIBG - Primary: Defence of Canada/North America (expertise: Arctic operations); Secondary: peacekeeping (PK), internal security (IS), limited war, ACE Mobile Force (Land).
>
> 2 CIBG - Primary: PK, IS, limited War (expertise: tropical operations); Secondary: Defence of Canada/North America, ACE Mobile Force (Land)
>
> 3 CIBG - Primary: NATO Europe (expertise: temperate environments); Secondary: Defence of Canada/North America, PK, IS, Limited War
>
> 4 CIBG - Primary: NATO Europe (expertise: nuclear warfare); Secondary: PK, IS, Limited War

Finally, there was the planned Commando Regiment, which was to be optimized for peacekeeping, internal security and limited war.

The general FMC concept of operations in a non-NATO theatre is revealing. The Commando Regiment, which later evolved into the Canadian Airborne Regiment, would secure a 'Mobile Command Overseas Base'. Strategic airlift and sealift would move one of the brigades to the disembarkation zone, while tactical airlift - a mixture of helicopters and light transports - would move it forward to the area of operations. Tactical air support would operate from the Overseas Base to support the terrestrial forces. Essentially, the Canadian Forces would select the brigade group closest

*Canadian armoured vehicles being loaded aboard a North Star transport aircraft*

Iwo Jima-*class helicopter carrier*

to the anticipated level of force required for the operation, and the FMC process would deploy, support, and operate it.

**Re-capitalization: The Perennial Challenge**

The planned structure of FMC was ambitious in equipment acquisition. Since the former RCAF's existing CF-104 Starfighter nuclear strike aircraft were not suited to FMC operations, a number of alternatives were explored. Among these were A-6 Intruders and F-4 Phantoms, but cost led Defence Minister Paul Hellyer towards the CF-5, a light strike fighter that could operate from less than ideal runways in the Third World. The planned 'air truck' - an idea that emerged from battlefield nuclear planning in the 1950s - became the basis for Buffalo and Caribou light transport aircraft, of which several squadrons would be required. Expansion of the C-130 Hercules force for tactical logistics operations (not strategic deployment or sustainment) was deemed essential. Several squadrons worth of helicopters - particularly the UH-1 Iroquois and the Sea Knight (called the Voyageur in Canadian service) - were part of the shopping list.

Strategic lift to the theater of operations was to be a combination of strategic airlift involving American-made C-141 Starlifters and amphibious landing ships. FMC planning even included input from the maritime force. Proposals to purchase two *Iwo Jima*-class landing platform/helicopter carriers, one for each coast, were raised. Canadian ship designs included helicopter carriers, landing platform docks with wet wells, and even a catamaran "heliporter". The most technically ambitious program was the proposed vertical take-off and landing (VTOL) aircraft. Called the Dynavert, and built by Canadair, this tilt-wing tactical transport pre-dated the American V-22 Osprey by a couple of decades. Several Dynavert prototypes were built and troop trials conducted. The intent was to operate the novel design from a heliporter-type ship or from one of the landing platforms.

There are many reasons why the Canadian Forces of the 21st century are not operating a jet-powered descendent of Dynavert (from the deck of a second-generation landing platform docks built in Canadian shipyards) in order to deploy the Commando Regiment in a situation short of war designed to support Canadian policy. First, the Pearson government refused to coordinate its fiscal policy effectively. Its finance minister took on the aspects of a rogue minister and refused to pay for the defence policy - a stall tactic that lasted until the next election. Public outcry over the merger of the three services and the creation of a single uniform took centre stage over the other beneficial aspects of the policy. This lead to the lateral transfer of the supportive minister.

The change of government in 1968 radically challenged Canada's traditional foreign and defence policy; Canada's place in the global power system was questioned and undermined by those in the Trudeau government. This put an end to all of the capital projects that were not already underway, leaving Canada with a surfeit of CF-5s and a few helicopters, but no strategic airlift or sealift. The brigade groups could train for their new tasks, but they could not get to where they needed to go. The need for intervention in the Third World was not on the priority list of the Trudeau Government, which favoured the expansion of the Canadian International Development Agency (CIDA), as well as the coddling of dictators, as opposed to their removal.

*Canadian Dynavert VTOL aircraft*

Even the concept of FMC was gone by the 1970s. The services re-emerged; first Maritime Command, and then Air Command in 1975. FMC moved away from a joint intervention force to being the army in waiting. Inter-service rivalry re-asserted itself as FMC lost its air assets to Air Command. The maritime forces were content to hunt submarines.

The only time FMC was ever employed overseas in a crisis remotely resembling its Situations Short of War mandate was Operation LEAVEN in 1967. Canada's UN contingent in Egypt was being held hostage by the Nasser government. A Canadian naval task group was deployed to the Mediterranean to assist in a planned evacuation, which would have involved part of a brigade group flown in to secure a withdrawal point for the UN Emergency Force (UNEF). The deployment of the naval task group was a factor in Nasser's decision to back off and let transport aircraft evacuate the Canadian contingent before hostilities with Israel began.

## Conclusion

What are the implications of the Forces Mobile Command odyssey for today?

- A warning: FMC of the 1960s tells us a lot but should not be used as a carbon-copy model for today's and tomorrow's force structure.

- Change may have to be forced on the three services whether they like it or not. This will be necessary, as the needs of the country to project power are more important than the priorities and concerns of individual services.

- Re-structuring is a long-term challenge. Some things do not change, no matter what the government of the day thinks. The Canadian military will have to be globally deployable, and will operate in coalitions in nasty places.

- The Canadian military needs to provide the political leadership with force options. Ottawa must not be allowed to settle for a narrow range of options based on short-term domestic political expediency because they do not know what they will need in the future.

- Strike the right balance between static requirements and mobile requirements.

- Beware the voices saying that Canada can contract out strategic transport to the private sector. The unhappy fate of UNEF in 1967 illustrates the necessity of having your own means of extracting your forces at short notice.

## Notes:

[1] This presentation is distilled from a two-part series: "Global Mobile: Flexible Response, Peacekeeping and the Origins of Forces Mobile Command, 1958-1964," The Army Doctrine and Training Bulletin Vol. 3 No. 3 Fall 2000 and "Global Mobile II: The Development of Forces Mobile Command, 1965-1972," The Army Doctrine and Training Bulletin Vol. 4 No. 2 Summer 2001.

# QUESTION & ANSWER FORUM

**Bruce Johnson, EADS Canada**

I want to comment on Professor Bland's presentation. We in the defence community are all able to visualize the capability that Canada strives for, but it is really difficult to articulate that vision in a fashion that either the government or the public at large can be made to understand. When I was with Northrop-Grumman, one of my colleagues, who worked in the electronic warfare field asked me, "Bruce, doesn't the air force realize the importance of modern electronic warfare in the modern fighter aircraft?" I replied, "Do not forget, there is no place they [Canadian aircraft] have to go." Consider the procurement for a new CF-18 targeting pod, to which $200-million was allocated in 2002. It went through the Treasury Board in 2003, and we have still yet to see a draft request for proposal (RFP) for the procurement. This tells you there is no sense of urgency for that capability in that aircraft because, presumably, there is no place they have to go. If you go back to the Gulf War, we carefully selected the operating area of the ships based on the capability of the task group. We could tailor their task to their capability.

I was struck by the analogy of the police force in Toronto. In Ottawa, the police force asks for more money, and generally speaking it gets more money, and of course, the people not only know what the police do, they know it does for them. If the CF stopped doing everything they do today, the only thing Canadians would notice missing would be search and rescue. Everything else seems to be involve going somewhere else to do things for other people; it ranks up there with the foreign aid discussion. I think for many, many years our discussion in this whole area has been going in the wrong direction, because when you are looking at discretionary capability it is very difficult to convince Canadians to pony up the funding.

**Sunil Ram, American Military University/Defence Studies Committee, RCMI**

This is a general question, but directed at Mark Sedra. The idea of 3-D, in my opinion, is cute but unrealistic. The fact is that some of the problems of 3-D that Mr. Sedra mentioned will not go away. The fact is that there is a part of the Department of Foreign Affairs and CIDA that have staked out their territory in these failed state scenarios, so that civil-military relations are problematic. So what other options does the government offer other than 3-D? Is there even any other thinking in the Department of Foreign Affairs or CIDA in that area, or are they tied to this 3-D approach?

**Mark Sedra**

I also tend to question the 3-D concept in terms of how it is conceived right now. In many respects, it is at a stage of promoting more intensive dialogue, but is that much different from what existed prior to 3-D in terms of communication between the departments? The process needs to be formalized and encourage greater inter-departmental communication by creating some standing bodies to foster and solidify these connections. But the reality is that not every player has an equal voice on every issue. The structures are just being established and there needs to be more time for these to be developed. I don't think you can change behaviour without changing structures. The current structures, if they are not altered, will perpetuate the same protective behaviours in terms of turf, budget, mandates, and so on. It is a part of changing this culture and moving this agenda forward.

**Alain Pellerin, Conference of Defence Associations**

One thing that struck me by Mr. Sedra's presentation was his depiction of the Provincial Reconstruction Team (PRT) in Khandahar that illustrated 250 military personnel, but only one from CIDA and one from Foreign Affairs Canada. The impression one gets from this is that 3-D has really only one pillar - defence - and the others do not really care. Is that the message?

**Dr. Sean Maloney, Royal Military College of Canada**

Can I address that? I have visited PRTs in Feyzabad and Kunduz to see how the Germans have it set up. I think we need to look away from counting the numbers and look at what the PRTs are actually for. There are different types of PRTs that do different things, but their primary focus is to collect information, centralize that information and move it to a provincial-level committee chaired by the governor. There is a lot of coordination of activities and, because of the terrain in Afghanistan, you are dealing with a lot of communications issues to which the military communication structure is better suited. So I would not look strictly at numbers to determine where the relative importance lies among the pillars within the PRTs.

In Kunduz the Germans had an ambassador-level foreign affairs individual and he had one CIDA equivalent and then there were 700 soldiers. That did not lessen his effectiveness and it did not lessen his influence in the system. Because the personalities worked really well together in that remote zone they were able to do their job effectively. But what is the objective? The objective is to assist the governor. We are not running the show there.

**Colonel Pellerin**

I would have thought there would be more from CIDA in particular because there is already some suspicion of the military from the NGO community. I think that is because of a lack of communication and understanding of what each is supposed to do.

**Dr. Maloney**

Let me be blunt. The purpose of all of this is to be able to counter the bad guys and gather enough information to assist the governor in deploying his monies effectively to ensure the population stays onside. Whether we are talking military or civilian, we are there for one purpose: to help rebuild and stabilize Afghanistan. You cannot separate the military and civilian components the way CIDA and the NGOs tend to do, otherwise we are back to this problem of stove-piping. That is a cultural issue with the NGOs and CIDA that is going to have to change whether they like it or not because they will not be permitted to coordinate their activities in these areas unless they change. NGOs who stray outside the fold get shot, eviscerated, and hung from trees. This is a true synergy and certain people in Ottawa are going to have to get their heads around that and stop separating the military dimension from the civilian.

**Mr. Sedra**

I would also say that one of the reasons that the military contingent would be so robust at this stage compared to the civilian component is because, particularly in Khandahar where Canadian Forces will be deployed, it is not yet a permissive environment that would enable a larger civilian component. One of the main purposes for the military is to provide a security umbrella so that civilian actors can operate effectively, and also, as was said, to extend the authority and legitimacy of the central government in these areas. Where there is a security vacuum, of course military forces play a vital role in extending that authority and legitimacy. One of the keys to this approach is that, over time, some of the PRT's will become civilianized and Afghanized. You have to see this heavy military factor as a stage in the process. Right now, responding to existing security conditions, which are still quite adverse, requires a more robust military component. Over time you might be able to augment this with a greater presence of both civilian and government agencies, but also NGOs and other civil society actors.

**Khanh Lekim, CISS member**

I would like to congratulate the CF and General Hillier who are doing an excellent job despite their hands being tied. We have done the impossible. But I would ask the leadership of Canada how we are going to play a role in the UN reform, human rights reform, and UN Security Council reform.

**Professor Douglas Bland, Queen's University**

Be quiet and give no cause for alarm.

**Major-General (Retd) Lewis Mackenzie**

I wonder if I could answer that last question very quickly. There will be no Security Council reform. If you read the UN charter, the veto of the permanent five members not only applies to issues of international peace and security; it also applies to procedure. Those that aspire to permanent status and veto - Japan, Germany, Brazil and India - have spent the last two years going around the world trying to convince people they should be allowed to join. They issued a statement in the early summer of 2005 saying they would revisit the problem in 15 years. They are not going to get it.

Second, David, in your opening comments you indicated that there was, if I remember the quote correctly, no link between failed states and terrorism. I think that it is more serious than that. There is a link between our interventions in failed states and terrorism. The *mujahideen* - Muslim militants who fight outside of their native country - arrived in Bosnia in the summer of 1992, and they are still there and they are expanding and running training bases. Afghanistan is another area that qualifies.

Third, I do not want to come across as sarcastic regarding the PRT by any stretch because they are going to do great work. But the work of the two foreign affairs officers, the one CIDA officer and two members of the RCMP is what used to be done by the Lieutenant we called the [civil-military cooperation (CIMIC)] officer in all the other missions we have been on. So I really think that probably a little bit more robust representation by the other two pillars would be justified.

It is an indication of where the world has things backwards, and I have been pleading this case for the last 10 years with no result. We always send in the NGOs, the nation-builders, to reconstruct a society before the killing stops. This is exactly what is happening in Darfur. So the PRTs going out into some of those very dangerous areas before the killing stops obviously require a very robust defence capability. I am not trying to be critical of the PRT. I am being critical of the dysfunction of the Security Council's sequence of deployment. The only thing they can get unanimity on is some sort of humanitarian intervention. As a result, we end up feeding the very people that are doing the killing because that is where the medicine goes to, and that is where the goods go to. When the humanitarian aid was flown into Sarajevo, 80 percent of it ended up on the black market or with the people doing the killing, and the UN High Commission for Refugees told me that was a good percentage. Only 20 percent going to the people who need the aid was extremely positive according to them. I rest my case. We have the sequence wrong.

**Julie Lindhout, President, Atlantic Council of Canada**

I agree with Lew Mackenzie about the priorities that need to be assigned when dealing with failed and failing states. But I do believe the 3-D approach is ultimately the right approach, although it may need a lot of refining. When we look at the situation in the world today and consider what all of the foreign aid has accomplished in Africa and elsewhere, I think the one element that needs to be recognized is the strong link between foreign aid and the creation of economic prosperity in the receiving country. That is the only way you can elevate the need for foreign aid. But economic stability is linked completely with the notion of political stability and safety and security for which there is a major role for the defence pillar. So at the moment I don't see the composition of a PRT as being disproportionate.

The one area that I think the development aspect needs to focus on much more is involving more local people rather than a lot of foreign NGOs doing the majority of the work. This would allow the local populations to benefit more from the money that is being sent out. The possibility of gaining more economic comfort and prosperity is the only solution to under-development and instability.

**Mr. Sedra**

I have just a couple of comments on the two recent interventions. Regarding the issue of civilian actors, and the premature entry of NGOs, to use the Afghan context, where institutions have been shattered, where all development indicators are abysmally low, there is a need for some immediate action. There is also a low-level insurgency that necessitates military support to provide both cover and support for those actions. But I think there is a need for some simultaneity between development, diplomacy and defence in this environment. I do think that the 3-D approach is a good one. I think these types of threats and the different aspects we are trying to confront in failed states - security elements, issues of governance and development - require a 3-D approach. In the cases of failed states, a lack of development and insufficient governance are causes of insecurity, which means they have to be linked to the intervention efforts. But I think you are entirely right to say as we try to implement these types of policies we have to keep local ownership in mind. This is about providing the local actors with the capacity to take responsibility for their own security, helping them establish a monopoly on the use of force, and helping them gain the capability to provide services to the population to alleviate poverty. So I think that capacity-building and local ownership are certainly things that have to be kept in mind for all the pillars.

**Major Kevin Brown, CISS Member**

My comment is for Mr. Sedra. You alluded to the army's poor assessment of past interventions and practices. In the army we have the lessons learned process that starts with after-action reviews and carries on with post-exit reports, of which I have written many. The biggest one I had to write was in 2002 as the operations officer for the 2nd battalion of the Royal 22nd Regiment deployed to Bosnia with SFOR. We wrote down everything that we had done in the five phases of the deployment. Did you not come across any similar mechanisms in any of the other agencies in your studies of 3-D and joined-up government?

**Mr. Sedra**

I agree that this analysis is going on in the different departments, but as I said the analysis is stove-piped, often not shared, not disseminated; it often does not reach the people who need it at the right times. There are cultural issues, there are secrecy issues, and perhaps a lack of willingness to share that information. I know that recently we have been discussing doing some lessons learned work within Foreign Affairs Canada on past interventions in failed states and complex development situations and so on. We really had to dig up some of the work which in all cases was not that easy to get. Part of this still has to do with vertical lines of management, departmentalism and so on, because there are no channels to provide that information in a timely manner. I am not disputing that the work is being done. It is just not being shared and exploited effectively.

**Prof. Bland**

The defence policy statement, the CDS's vision, and the work that has been going on over the last few months is important, bold, and will carry the armed forces forward. It is the long-delayed response to the post-Cold War era that we are in. A lot of people thought when we went to Somalia and Bosnia these were one-off situations, and as soon as we got out of there we would go back to proper soldiering. It took almost 10 years for enough people who commanded at various rank levels and had experience in those operations to realize that situations like Somalia were not the exception - that this is the new situation and we have to change the Forces accordingly. But they have been trying to do it with a budget that was fixed in 1993, and with a force level fixed in 1993. In a business I do not think one would put forward a vision to shareholders that did not have a business plan and that did not have a budget that matched what they are going to try to do. It is not the CDS's place to set the budget, but that is a weakness in the recent policy.

My bigger concern is that we now need to have the second shoe drop. We need a post-Cold War system of defence administration to produce the forces that we need for these operations - in other words, to support the CDS and the people who are working to reform the armed forces. We do not currently have that. In fact, there is great resistance to doing that. When former defence minister John McCallum put out the Management Efficiency Study - in which he wanted to look at reallocating things within the defence portfolio - he met great resistance from senior officials within the department. When McCallum left the portfolio, the report was taken off the website the next day.

The conceptual framework for defence administration was set out in 1972. It is a Cold War anachronism and if we are only going to have limited funds you have to find someway to take those very limited funds to produce the outcome you want. Right now the resources - people, money, equipment - are not aimed in that direction, and that is where we need to go.

**Phillip Richardson, CIIA Member**

I think the question before us is how do we bring this defence policy to life. How can those who believe in a stronger military with a sense of itself hold the government's feet to the fire? How can it mobilize public opinion? We know the military in Canada does not have a strong domestic constituency, which is why it was cut so freely by this government over the last generation or so. So I think it is up to us, people interested in this, to publicize what is discussed here.

I believe one of the parliamentary committees is holding hearings on the policy statement, but there has not been as part of this process much public participation. In fact this has largely been an elitist exercise. But there is hard work to be done here. I worry about stamina and staying power in this. A lot of people think that Defence Minister Bill Graham has the gravitas in Cabinet to push this through, and if he leaves that may not be so. There is of course great worry about the money being there. I think it is incumbent upon us to raise awareness, bring Canadians into this discussion.

I am not so sure that I see the larger vision that might be here, and I certainly do not see the words from the government mobilizing the public and reaching out to Canadians in a way it might. That has a lot to do with how the policy statement arrived. As David Rudd said, it unfortunately arrived the day the Pope died. But there was not a lot of selling done from Ministers or the Prime Minister. I think we lost an opportunity, which sadly is not uncommon in Canada.

**Larry Herman, CIIA member**

We have a forward-looking defence policy statement integrated into a larger foreign policy goal with lots of ideas about implementation. We in the defence policy community, I think, should put a positive view forward about it. If we do not do it, how do you expect the general public to do it? I am suggesting there are many important parts in this statement that are visionary and worthy of public support, and it is up to the defence community to do a bit of selling and not to be constantly criticizing what has happened in the past.

# THE PROCUREMENT CYCLE'S RACE WITH OBSOLESCENCE 1960-2005

## General (Retd) Paul Manson

On 17 May, 1977 I was called out of a French class in Quebec City, where I was attending the year-long Federal Biculturalism Program, to take an urgent call from National Defence Headquarters (NDHQ). To my great surprise I was informed that the Cabinet had approved the acquisition of a new fleet of Fighter aircraft, and that I was to move to Ottawa immediately to run the procurement. At that time it was the largest capital equipment program in the history of the Canadian Government, at $2.34-billion in 1975 dollars.

Four days later I was on the job, having discovered that I had been assigned no staff, no offices, nor even an approved Statement of Operational Requirement. But in spite of these and countless other challenges along the way, including two changes of government, a mere three years later a contract was signed with McDonnell Douglas for the purchase of 138 CF-18 Hornet aircraft. Production began immediately, and the first Hornet was delivered to the air force in November of 1983; only six years after the project start-up.

Now, fast forward to the present and the sad story of the Maritime Helicopter Project (MHP). Initiated in the mid-1980s, this project will not produce operational ship-borne helicopters until 2010 at the earliest - almost 30 years later.

I was also involved in the helicopter procurement, but in a very different way. In 1993 I was President of Paramax, the Montreal company which held the contract for the design and integration of all the on-board electronics systems for the EH-101 helicopter, which a year earlier had been selected by the Mulroney Government for both the ship-borne and search-and-rescue roles. To our great

---

**Gen (Retd) Paul Manson** is President of the Conference of Defence Associations Institute (CDAI) and a former Chief of Defence Staff.

dismay, the contract was terminated by Jean Chrétien within hours of being sworn in as prime minister. That decision, which has been compared with the cancellation of the Avro Arrow 35 years earlier, forced me to lay off more than 750 employees the following day, and it set the maritime helicopter procurement back by at least 15 years.

These two examples, the New Fighter Aircraft and the MHP, appear to reinforce the common perception that there has been inordinate growth in procurement times for military equipment in Canada over the past several decades. Indeed, the system was called "insane" by University of Calgary professor David Bercuson in a recent article.

This broad-based concern, both within and outside of the armed forces, raises several important questions which I would like to examine. First, is the perceived growth real? Second, if it is, what are the causes? Third, what are the consequences for the Canadian Forces? Fourth, what needs to be done about it?

Before delving into these questions, I would like to place the situation in the context of the current state of defence in this country. I retired as Chief of Defence Staff in 1989, just months before the fall of the Berlin Wall and the collapse of the Soviet bloc. The intervening years have seen huge changes in the global strategic scene and the Canadian military's reaction to the "New World Order." In spite of a 25% reduction in the Canadian Forces (CF) personnel strength since 1990, the operational tempo has increased dramatically, with frequent deployments to such overseas locations as the former Yugoslavia, the Persian Gulf, Haiti, Somalia and East Timor. Meanwhile the CF have frequently been called upon for assistance in urgent domestic situations such as the ice storm, floods, forest fires and the 2002 G8 Summit Meeting in Kananaskis. And then there was the demanding aftermath of 9/11 with the military dispatched to Afghanistan.

To cope with the changing strategic and technological landscape, it is generally acknowledged that the CF must undergo a major paradigm shift, from a Cold War posture to one of continuous operations in multiple locations. This so-called "transformation" is in fact already underway, and an important element of it is the need to provide the three services with the right sort of equipment to meet the demands of current and future operations.

Unfortunately, this is not going well. Major

Gen (Retd) Paul Manson

reductions in the defence budget in the 1990s left insufficient capital funds for the purchase of new systems at a time when the rust-out of old equipment was the norm.

With this brief background, I would like now to examine the first question by asking: "How much growth has there been in the procurement cycle over the years?"

To find the answer, a study was conducted of the procurement history of major capital equipment going back to about 1960. It was first necessary to find an acceptable definition of "procurement cycle" in order to allow meaningful comparisons. In the figures provided, for want of a better definition, the baseline for comparison is the time from Cabinet go-ahead to Initial Operational Capability (IOC). The latter term is commonly used and understood, but the former is rather arbitrary. In some cases, Cabinet go-ahead was not that clear-cut, but in all cases we were able to provide reasonable dates for the purposes of comparison.

One should note, however, that Cabinet approval is almost always preceded by a lengthy process of developing operational requirements and seeking approval for the same within the Department of National Defence (DND). In other words, the real timelines are considerably longer than what is evident from the figures.

We decided also to limit our investigation to a manageable and representative number of Major Crown Projects (MCP), beginning with those which received Government go-ahead during the Cold War years. These include:

- CF-5 Freedom Fighter
- CC-130 Hercules Transport Aircraft
- M113 Armoured Personnel Carrier
- DDH280 Class Destroyer (four ships)
- Leopard C1 Main Battle Tank
- Tribal Class Update & Modernization Program (four ships)
- Long Range Maritime Patrol Aircraft (18 Auroras)
- New Fighter Aircraft (138 CF-18 Hornet aircraft)
- Canadian Patrol Frigate Phases I & II (six ships each)
- Tactical Command, Control & Communications System
- Maritime Helicopter Program (originally NSA/NSH)

Figure 1 illustrates the resulting plot of procurement duration versus calendar year for these projects. It shows what appears to be a pronounced growth in procurement cycle time that is more or less linear if you discount the anomalous MHP. (Including the MHP makes the growth appear exponential.)

So the growth is real, and it is substantial. But that is not the whole story.

Next we plotted the post-1990 major procurements, namely the Light Armoured

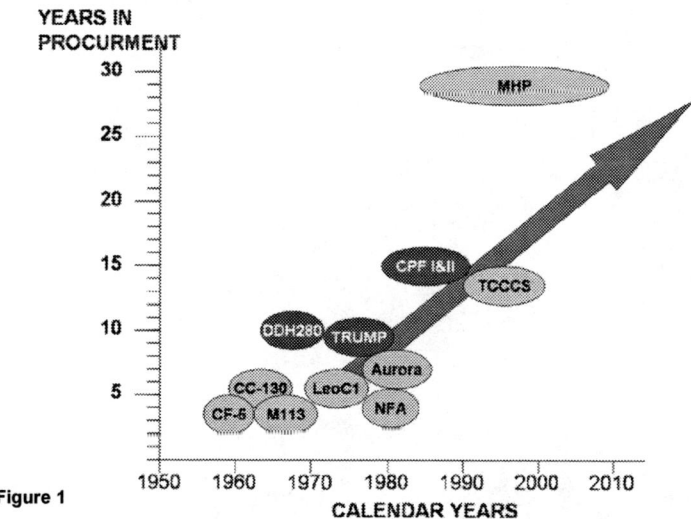

Figure 1

Vehicle (LAV-3), the Griffon tactical support helicopter, and the CC-150 Polaris transport aircraft, which is based on the Airbus A-310. The results are shown in Figure 2. It is interesting to note that these last three programs were all brought in relatively quickly.

So what conclusions can we draw from the plot of procurement times? The first is that there is indeed an upward trend in the time taken to complete major capital equipment programs for the Canadian military - in some cases to an alarming extent. Upon further examination, however, the plot reveals an interesting story, as shown in Figure 3. Note that there appears to be three categories of project with quite different procurement times.

The bottom zone includes a number of equipment programs that were brought to fruition reasonably quickly (i.e. eight years or less from start to finish). The interesting thing to note is that these were all basically "off-the-shelf" purchases from existing production lines in Canada or abroad.

Looking at the middle band - in the case of the Tribal-class destroyer (DDH), the destroyer update and modernization program (TRUMP) and the Canadian Patrol Frigate (CFP) - these capital ship acquisitions were all specifically designed for the Canadian Navy, and constructed in Canadian shipyards. Together with the tactical radio program (TCCCS), which was also designed to Canadian specifications and built in Canada, the procurement cycle varied from 8-16 years. The Aurora maritime patrol aircraft was a version of the Lockheed Orion customized for Canadian use. Note that it shows consistency with the pattern, in that it falls on the border between the first two categories.

The unfinished MHP is in a category all by itself, having been the victim of politi-

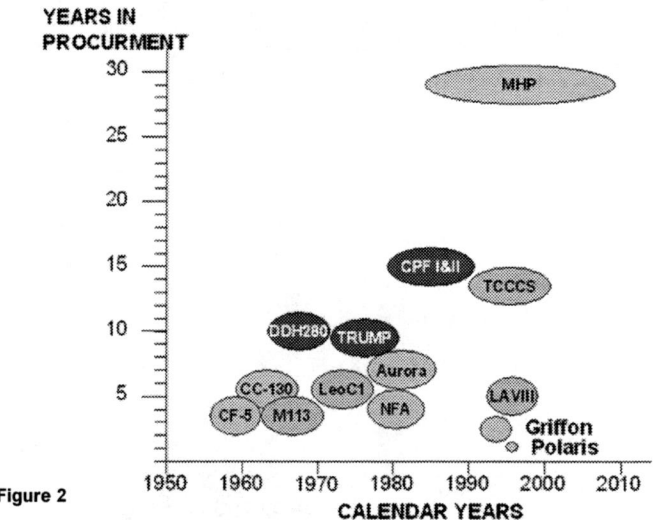

Figure 2

cal interference and legal wrangling, plus a measure of customization (or "Canadianization"). The basic helicopter was essentially off-the-shelf, but the on-board systems, accounting for about 50 percent of the cost, were newly designed to meet Canadian specifications.

These observations lead to an important conclusion: that the duration of a military procurement is very sensitive to the degree of Canadianization.

That, of course, is not the whole story. The formal procurement process has often been cited as having become overly bureaucratic and time-consuming. Much of this growth has occurred within DND, which has worked very hard to ensure that taxpayers' money spent on new equipment produces results that are operationally effective and financially efficient. Over the past 40 years or so, increasingly detailed procedures have evolved, each of which might be justified in its own right, but which in their totality have evolved into a cumbersome and time-consuming process. A measure of DND's search for perfection is that by 1997 there were no fewer than 1,200 qualified program management personnel in the department. The fact that this number had fallen to 500 by 2004 was an unwanted development related to government-mandated force reductions and personnel shortages.

To be fair, a lot of the growth in the DND process is a response to external pressures. Media scrutiny of DND re-equipment programs has become increasingly intense. Bad publicity leads to public disfavour and puts government approval at risk. Delays or even project cancellation (as in the case of the EH-101 helicopter) are real possibilities. In this environment, risk-taking is discouraged and perfect solutions are sought, but at a price in terms of the time to completion.

Much of the bureaucratic processes are beyond DND's control. Over the years

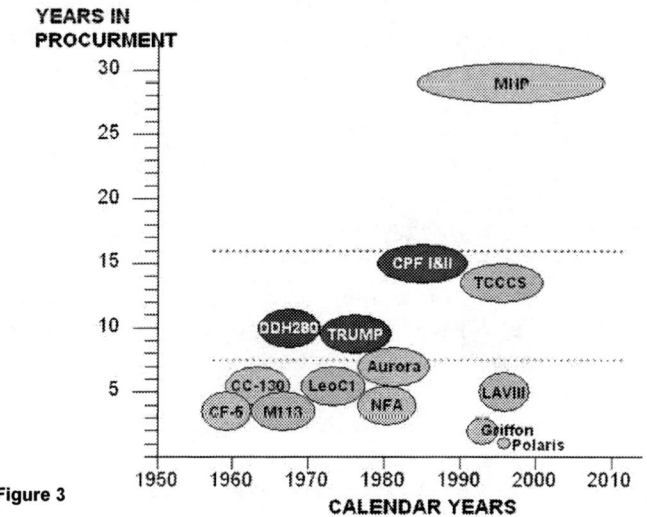
Figure 3

there has emerged a complex system of inter-departmental reviews which must be catered to by DND. Failure to satisfy the particular needs of other federal departments can lead to inordinate delays. Just scheduling inter-departmental meetings can be frustratingly difficult.

An oft-quoted case in point is the development of Industrial Regional Benefits (IRB) requirements over the years as a thorn in the side of DND. IRBs are the non-military industrial requirements that must be satisfied in order to award a contract. They may involve the requirement of setting up a production facility in a certain region of the country (even if it is not cost-effective to do so) or dividing work between several regions, thereby driving up the per unit cost of the item to be acquired. They may also involve offset agreements, whereby the winning bidder is obliged to purchase non-defence goods made in Canada. The IRBs adds to the complexity of the procurement process, but I believe that, on average, they have not been a major factor in procurement cycle growth. But because they are politically sensitive, there is always a danger they could mire down a given program.

A more substantial question is the debilitating impact of the budgetary system on procurement times. Each year, like other government departments, DND is assigned a total budget allocation which includes specific amounts for personnel, operations, and maintenance on the one hand, and capital on the other. Although it is possible to transfer money from one area to the other, this is a difficult and time-consuming process, which reduces flexibility in the management of equipment programs.

Also, the arbitrary threshold of $100-million for MCP leads to inefficiencies in the procurement process. Because MCPs must go through a more difficult and time-consuming approval process, DND has on occasion broken otherwise coherent equipment programs into a series of smaller projects, each of which is under the $100-million threshold. Administering a larger number of smaller acquisitions is obviously inefficient; it imposes a heavy burden on the procurement staff, with a predictable and adverse impact on acquisition time and cost.

Let us re-visit the final two questions posed earlier: "What are the consequences of procurement cycle growth", and; "What can be done about it?"

Clearly, a slowing down of the procurement process can and does have the most serious implications for the military. The forced extension of ancient equipment (already more than 30 years old in many cases) means a worsening capacity for effective operations and added risks for our men and women in uniform. The cost of maintaining older equipment like the Sea King helicopter, to cite an egregious example, is a heavy drain on the defence budget, which means less money for new equipment. Meanwhile, program management costs for the drawn-out replacement programs are also adding up. The net result is a vicious circle of diminishing returns.

With the Canadian military attempting to transform itself to meet the demands of a rapidly changing world, it is simply untenable to take 10-15 years to introduce new systems into the inventory. Surely the turgid pace of capability acquisition is a barrier that stands between the status quo and a transformed military. It goes without saying that the CF must have the right equipment at the right time if they are to meet the operational demands of the new strategic and tactical environments.

Look also at the impact on industry of 10-year-plus procurement times. Time is money to companies in the defence sector, and it is frustrating for them to have to cater to the inclusion, for example, of a so-called definition phase which can impose an additional six to eight months of work on the competing firms. This adds to the cost of competing and to the risk, since only the winning company will have the opportunity of recouping the extra expense, which it will do by charging DND (and the taxpayer) more than it otherwise would have.

For the firms competing in a given acquisition, keeping highly qualified industrial teams together and occupied while the government goes through lengthy internal processes is difficult, risky and expensive. Again, it is the Canadian taxpayer who ultimately pays the cost.

And here is another troubling consequence of the situation. As seen through the eyes of an off-shore corporation, Canada's excessively lengthy procurement process is a disincentive for investing in high technology in this country.

So what can be done? One can draw an important conclusion: that Canadianization of new military systems should be avoided if at all possible, since this adds years to the cycle. The days when Canada could afford such luxury are long past. Fortunately, with major advances in standardization, and with the availability of a wide range of existing systems on the market, there should rarely be a need for the CF to opt for the design of Canadian-specific systems.

A second conclusion also emerges: that the administrative process must be streamlined wherever possible, even if this means accepting a reasonable measure of risk-taking.

This is not to say, however, that fast procurement is impossible in the existing system. As demonstrated in Figure 3, it is possible to work within the system to achieve a procurement cycle time of under 10 years provided the complexities that tend to plague the process are avoided.

Lest you believe that this is too much to hope for, consider what happened in this country during the Second World War. As historian Jack Granatstein has pointed out in a recent monograph, between 1939 and 1945 the federal government and industry worked together in this country to produce 16,000 military aircraft, 410 merchant ships plus several hundred warships, 3,500 battle tanks, and 800,000 military vehicles of various kinds. To be sure, the technology of that era was less complex, but all of this, and much more, was accomplished from a cold start in just six years, and at a time when Canada's population was only one-third of today's.

Surely, then, we can do better than we have been doing in providing timely new equipment for our military.

# MISSING IN ACTION: A DEFENCE-INDUSTRIAL STRATEGY FOR CANADA

## Peter Boag

**Introduction**

I am very pleased to be able to provide an industry perspective on the recently released International Policy Statement, which the Government of Canada has described as "Canada's first comprehensive and integrated foreign policy framework".

The International Policy Statement (IPS) acknowledges and is founded on several important realities: that Canadian defence and security policy must be centered on a strong Canada-US defence relationship; that in this fast-shrinking and dangerous global village, security in Canada ultimately begins with stability abroad, and; that we need to expand, transform and integrate the Canadian Forces (CF) to ensure that they are more effective, more relevant and more responsive in the security environment of the 21st century.

Looking specifically at the defence component of the IPS, and from the perspective of the Aerospace Industries Association of Canada (AIAC), the government generally got it right. In terms of principles and priorities, and men and materiel; modernizing the CF-18 weapons systems; building a tactical and strategic airlift, both fixed and rotary wing; replacing the Buffalo and Hercules aircraft for search-and-rescue, and; modernizing the Aurora patrol aircraft, while developing unmanned air vehicles for coastal surveillance.

The IPS does, in the main, recognize what must be done. But certain deficiencies remain. A case in point: the parallel decision to stand down from participation in

---

**Peter Boag** is President and CEO of the Areospace Industries Association of Canada (AIAC).

ballistic missile defence (BMD), just months after we agreed to make NORAD the eyes and ears of the proposed BMD system.

The IPS was an attempt to bring together Canadian diplomatic, development, defence and commercial policies in a comprehensive and integrated fashion; the word "commerce" signifying the government's recognition of the increasingly intimate ties between trade and investment.

Peter Boag

Noticeable by its absence, however, was any discussion of the need for a comprehensive and integrated approach to "defence commerce", or the need to foster and maintain a domestic industrial base to ensure a secure supply of materiel and expertise for the execution of its international policies.

Indeed, the absence of any discussion of the strategic role of industry in meeting Canada's defence and security challenges, in developing and delivering capabilities to the CF, and in supporting them over their life cycles, was a glaring omission of the IPS. It is this concept of "defence commerce" and the need for a defence industrial strategy that I want to focus on - particularly as it pertains to the aerospace sector.

**Canada's Aerospace Industry**

Aerospace is one of Canada's remarkable industrial stories. Despite our small domestic market we have been able to build the world's fourth largest national aerospace industry.

Annual industry revenues are $22-billion - the vast bulk generated today in the civil aviation market serving foreign (that is to say, primarily American) customers. We employ some 75,000 talented and highly skilled Canadians. And unlike the automotive sector, which is located overwhelmingly along Highway 401 in the cities of Southern Ontario, aerospace is a truly pan-Canadian industry.

Key firms act as anchor tenants in various local and provincial economies from coast to coast. Indeed, it is not widely appreciated that the industry means as much to the economies of Winnipeg and Manitoba, as it does to those of Montreal and Quebec.

Canada's success in building a world-class aerospace sector was no accident or fluke. Rather, it was the result of a deliberate and intelligent partnership between private sector firms and Canadian governments. A key part of this was a defence industrial partnership one that contributed in no small way to the growth of Bombardier into the world's third largest producer of commercial aircraft; the establishment of CAE Ltd. as the world leader in commercial and defence simulation; the development of Pratt & Whitney Canada as a world leader in small gas turbine engines, and; the establishment CF fleet in-service support capabilities that have been the catalyst for the development of substantial export business opportunities. I speak here of companies like Standard Aero, IMP Group International Inc. and L-3 Spar.

Central to the success of the Canadian aerospace sector has been Canada's partnership with the United States in collective and cooperative defence and security arrangements, many of which have served to create a North American industrial base.

The foundation of this remarkable partnership was laid some 65 years ago with the formation of the Permanent Joint Board on Defence (PJBD) and the signing of the Hyde Park Agreement concerning joint Canada - US development and production of defence equipment. The Hyde Park Agreement was the precursor to a number of similar programs in future decades. Agreements like the Defence Production and Defence Development Sharing Arrangements (DPSA, DDSA) made Canadian-based firms an integral part of the North American industrial base.

Buying its major weapons systems from the United States became the cornerstone of Canadian defence procurement. From this a *quid pro quo* emerged. Favoured access to the much larger US defence market in return for shopping in the US became a key element of the Canadian defence industrial base strategy.

**Changing Times, New Challenges**

Over the past years, a series of decisions, events and neglect have weakened this all-important Canada-US dimension. Canada's defence spending was slashed, with deep cuts to procurement and defence research and development (R&D), leading to serious erosion of military capabilities. In turn, Canada, in the eyes of the US, lost its status as a credible military ally and defence industrial partner. As a consequence, a number of instruments began to wither (DDSA, for example) and new obstacles to co-operation arose, including restrictions on access to US technology and the US Department of Defense (DoD) market.

The AIAC believes that for Canadian-based firms, including Canadian subsidiaries of foreign-held firms, to be as successful in the future as they have been in the past, we need to recommit to a industrial base strategy that adequately protects the CF's security of supply, develops and provides access to key technologies, and enables Canada to participate in and influence strategic collaborations with its allies. Doing so requires that we strengthen and sustain a deliberate government-industry partnership here in Canada - one rooted in the realities of a fast-changing global marketplace.

This must be done in a way that recognizes certain realities - among them the continuing globalization of the industry. This phenomenon takes many forms. One is that a growing number of countries aspire to emulate Canada and build a national aerospace capability - most notably, Brazil, Japan, China and South Korea. Traditional domestic supply chains are disappearing, replaced by a global supply network.

A second dimension of globalization is that the industry continues to consolidate. We are witnessing an inexorable trend towards fewer, larger, international platforms and programs. This is a trend exemplified in the civil aviation sector by the sharing of risk between American, Japanese and European firms in the Boeing 787 commercial airliner project. In the military domain it is exemplified by the effective pooling of both risks and rewards in the multinational F-35 Joint Strike Fighter program, in which Canada is a Level 3 partner.

A second reality is the changing structure of the global industry. While it still generally comprises three tiers, the value proposition required of firms in each tier has changed.

Firms in the first tier are the still the prime contractors, but their role is increasingly that of "enabling architecture systems integrators", with an information-centric focus. This means that so-called "software competencies" are now the critical competitive discriminators. Tier 2 firms must be capable of devising, integrating and delivering complete aircraft and/or mission systems involving complex assemblies & structures. Tier 3 firms that produce simple systems and assemblies, proprietary products and equipment, "boards and chips", and specialty processes must enhance their cost structures, improve quality and become more flexible in responding to customer requirements.

A closely-linked trend is the intense and increasing competition in the global marketplace. This is characterized by:

- The constant demand from customers to provide "more for less" through continuous innovation - a market force cascading right down the supply chain;

- The intense competition among firms to secure a role in next generation supply chains, and the important life cycle support work that follows;

- The intense competition among governments to secure next generation investment, knowing that assembly and top tier system integration platforms act like magnets, thereby attracting investment by adjacent suppliers.

Another market reality is the political nature of the aerospace industry. As we all know, aerospace has always been an unavoidably political realm. It is the nature of the beast, given the many advanced technologies, safety concerns that drive rigorous regulations and standards, and the obvious national security/defence industrial base implications. The level of political intervention is, if anything, increasing, as the stakes grow larger and the world shrinks. This will have inevitable consequences for Canadian defence, security and commercial interests.

A case in point, which flows from the weakened Canada-US relationship and which directly threatens Canada's domestic industrial base, is an increasingly restrictive American export controls regime.

In the late 1990s the US State Department began to tighten controls on the export of US-origin goods and technologies that it considered could pose threats to its national security. Steps taken included removing the Canadian Exemption under the International Traffic in Arms Regulations (ITAR) that had permitted the export license-free transfer to Canadian companies of a broad range of goods and technologies that remained controlled in respect to transfers to other nations. License-free transfers to Canada had provided Canadian companies an advantage in acquiring technical data required to bid on US defence procurement opportunities and importantly, to engage in partnering and collaborative technology development with American firms. While the Canadian Exemption was reinstated, in part, in 2001, its scope is more limited. Perhaps of more significance is the resulting reluctance of US companies to exploit the full scope of the Canadian Exemption to make license-free transfer to Canada.

And despite US agreement to work towards expanding the scope of the exemption, things are getting worse, not better. Greater restrictions on the export of items on the Commerce Department's Commerce Control List (CCL) are now also being considered by the US government. As the items on the CCL encompass state-of-the art manufacturing equipment, materials processing and dual-use technologies, the implementation of more restrictive access controls will have a broadly and profoundly negative impact on the competitiveness and technology base of Canadian aerospace firms, as well as those in other advanced technology manufacturing sectors. To reverse the tide, we must be, and be seen to be in the eyes of the US, an effective contributor to the security of North America, and to bi-lateral or multi-lateral interventions where our foreign policy interests align.

A second case, which amply demonstrates the priority other nations place on developing and sustaining domestic defence industrial capability, and the degree to which they are prepared to intervene, was the engine selection for the European A400M transport aircraft. A Canadian-based firm, Pratt & Whitney Canada, had won the competition on the basis of a superior technical and financial solution, only to see this win overturned by political intervention at the highest level, and the contract awarded to a European consortium.

That's the world in which not just all Canadian, but all aerospace firms now live. And it's the reason why the AIAC has long sought a national aerospace strategy for Canada. A national strategy that we hope to develop in the months ahead through the recently-created vehicle of the Canadian Aerospace Partnership (CAP).

**Public-Private Partnerships: The Way Ahead**

Formed in April of 2005, CAP brings together the key actors in the aerospace industry - the federal government, governments in the key aerospace provinces of BC, Manitoba, Ontario, Quebec and Nova Scotia, senior aerospace executives from across the country, labour and academia.

The concept is simple. CAP is to be a forum for continuous engagement and dialogue among all key stakeholders, based on the realities of the global aerospace market as it is, not as we Canadians might like it to be. The goal is to create an ambitious but achievable strategic vision, with clear objectives and measurable targets; to assign roles and responsibilities, and; to agree on priorities so we optimize the opportunities ahead.

To realize its goals, CAP has assigned initial priority to three issues and established focused working groups for each, with reports due in the summer of 2005. Each of these working groups is examining issues that have direct relevance to Canada's defence industrial base.

One working group is focused on next generation platforms and the role Canadian leadership or participation in these international programs plays in creating long-term growth opportunities for the industry.

The task of this working group is to develop a framework and supporting processes that will enable Canadian industry and governments to make appropriate co-investment decisions on major new aerospace development programs - decisions that optimize individual and collective returns to Canada, including their contribution to developing essential defence industrial capabilities.

We are talking about both civil and military programs in both aviation and space - programs like the Boeing 787, the Airbus A380, Bombardier's CSeries, the Joint

Strike Fighter, Boeing's Multi-Mission Aircraft, the Galileo satellite, and projects that are just over the horizon, like the Boeing 737 and Airbus A320 successors.

What we need to do is devise an intelligent evaluation process to identify current and potential Canadian competencies that fit within current and potential programs, and to then execute a "capture strategy" that will optimize Canadian participation and returns in the identified opportunities.

A second working group is focused on a developing a strategy and enabling framework to induce a higher level of Canadian industry and government investment in aerospace technology development and facilitate its commercialization.

The goal is to identify mechanisms that will achieve a better balance between public and private investment across the full continuum of basic and applied research, technology development, demonstration and commercialization. This includes understanding the dual use (civil and military) nature of many technologies, and the pivotal role played by defence R&D in advanced technology economies around the world. This role is essential to developing and sustaining vital CF capabilities, and for which the output is often transferred to wider commercial applications outside the defence sector.

Today, defence R&D levels in Canada are frankly nothing less than pitiful. The US spends some US$70-billion annually in RDT&E. In comparison, annual budget of Defence Research and Development Canada (DRDC) is roughly $250-million. The numbers speak for themselves.

This leads me to CAP's third working group, which is focusing on Canadian procurement practices - particularly, but not exclusively, in the defence field. Its mandate is to propose a framework and enabling mechanisms for better harnessing and levering public sector procurement spending in a way that optimally balances the needs and interests of both government(s) and Canadian-based industry. Essential defence industrial capabilities are a key component of this work.

A crucial weakness of the current approach to defence capability acquisition and retention is the "boom and bust" environment created by a "project-by-project" procurement cycle. If we continue with the present unstructured approach there is no guarantee that Canada will have the defence industrial capabilities necessary to support implementation of the IPS.

We need to consider how Canada can more strategically leverage defence technology development and procurements to create an environment that will sustain a robust industrial capacity in Canada that can support foreign and defence policy goals. This will ensure that critical capabilities are retained - as losing and then recreating them will be costly and disruptive to achieving Canada's long-term objectives.

DND's preference for purchasing proven, "off-the-shelf" products regardless of national origin or Canadian economic impact has led it, somewhat ironically, to become the greatest proponent of free trade among all government departments. Departmental officials are loath to exercise Canada's NAFTA and WTO rights to exempt certain procurements from national security considerations.

In plain English, here's the crux of the matter as we see it at the AIAC. In sharp contrast to Canadian procurement practices and attitudes, both the US and the European Union (EU) consciously and constantly use defence spending to incubate and develop promising technologies for both strategic and competitive advantage. The A400M is but one example.

The US and EU think strategically and long-term, drawing the link between individual procurements and their domestic industrial base and economic interests. As a result of this asymmetrical approach, we have created a somewhat perverse situation here in Canada. DND's preference for off-the-shelf solutions creates an inherent bias in favour of those firms that have already secured prior American or European contracts - programs where customer-paid R&D often plays a major role in the commercialization of the product, so it is available "off the shelf" for Canadian use. American and European procurement practices in turn are skewed in favour of their own domestic suppliers. DND's preference for the low direct/upfront cost methodology tends to create an additional element of bias, since existing suppliers to US programs can price aggressively to secure this incremental Canadian business. The result is a *de facto* bias in Canadian defence procurement towards those American and European-based suppliers. This happens at the expense of Canadian-based firms, and with little or no concern about the long-term impacts on domestic industrial capability, or the broader definition of "value for money".

Indeed, if you ask a Canadian-based firm the best way to win a contract with DND, you will increasingly hear the same, cynical refrain. Do what you have to do to win a contract with the Pentagon, including migrating capability to become as American as possible. In other words, being American may help you in Washington, and won't hurt you at all in Ottawa. But for reasons outlined above, being Canadian may indeed hurt you in Washington, and it won't help you at all in Ottawa. And in this world of dual-use technologies, if migrating your military capability means your civilian application must follow, then so be it.

Let me be clear. We are not advocating blanket market protectionism and directed procurements without competition. We recognize the need to fully demonstrate value for taxpayers' money - although this is the norm for many of our major competitor nations. Nor are we advocating the unnecessary "Canadianization" of our defence purchases - the problem that Paul Manson spoke to earlier.
Rather, we seek fuller recognition that defence procurement has some unique characteristics that make it different from the commercial business. The

Department of National Defence is the sole customer of defence equipment and services in Canada. Every time it makes a decision to acquire a particular piece of equipment, whether from a domestic or foreign source, it effectively shapes the future of the aerospace and defence industry in Canada, with long-term impact on industry's ability to support CF operations at home and abroad, and on Canada's dual-use advanced technology base.

So, what does all this mean? AIAC recommends that in implementing the International and Defence Policy Statements, Canada must:

1. Develop a robust, coherent framework to enable early strategic decision-making on Canadian participation in new aerospace development programs. This framework should be supported by appropriate policy and analytical tools for assessing and evaluating overall Canadian benefits of participation, and by appropriate partnership models and support mechanisms.

2. Increase Canadian investment in aerospace technology development - in particular the important defence R&D component. It must maximize the impact of this investment by articulating a Canadian aerospace "Technology Vision" that designates key technology domains, and creates an industry/government/academia technology network that spans the full spectrum of Canadian aerospace technology development capability and infrastructure (commercial and defence) so that we can achieve maximum leverage through collaboration.

3. Create more effective mechanisms and processes to ensure earlier and more substantive consideration by cabinet ministers of how specific defence procurements can be leveraged to secure wider security and economic objectives, and enhance the competitiveness of Canadian industry.

4. More fully exercise Canada's negotiated trade rights in order to exempt selected, key procurements, thereby allowing the federal government to broaden the test of value for Canadian taxpayers. This means:

    - Developing inter-departmental mechanism for assessing case to invoke National Security Exemption;

    - Defining "national security" more broadly (i.e. beyond "national defence");

    - Recognizing to a greater degree "economic value-added" when assessing proposals from industry.

5. Leverage defence goods procured from foreign sources in a more strategic fashion to strengthen the technological, manufacturing and services provision capabilities of Canada's industrial base. This involves:

    - Focusing on quality versus quantity of industrial benefits placed by contractors;
    - Designating key technologies and service capabilities for placement of benefits.

6. Adopt a culture of risk-tolerance that promotes the incubation and first-use adoption of leading-edge technologies developed by Canadian-based firms. Of course, this carries with it the concomitant requirement to increase defence R&D budgets.

7. Embrace innovative solutions advanced by industry that reduce costs and improve the quality of service delivery when implementing new procurement and service delivery models. This would include the aggressive adoption of a performance-based acquisition approach for both goods and services.

8. Make available to industry more substantive information, and at an earlier stage, on National Defence's Capital Plan and upcoming procurements. Also, provide industry with greater transparency into how specific procurements are to be undertaken (from requirements definition to bid evaluation).

Underpinning all of this is the vital need to rebuild the relationship with the United States, to strengthen the notion of an integrated North American defence industrial base. Perhaps the most important reality is that Canada's defence procurement needs and budget will, at best, be modest. Hence for Canadian-base firms to grow and sustain capabilities essential to Canadians national security needs, they will need access to other markets.

## Conclusion

We can lay out an international policy that includes rebuilding the Canadian Forces so that it can meet the security challenges of the 21st century. What remains to be seen is whether the Government of Canada is prepared to act. Only time will tell if this and future governments will have the political will to truly harmonize Canadian foreign, defence and trade policies, or as we have so often seen in the past, allow short-term political interests (BMD, for example) to drive a wedge between these three elements that will constrain any ability to translate the words of the IPS into deeds and capabilities.

# SETTING OUR COURSE

## General R. J. Hillier

I arrived early today because I want to hear the way you are going to help us implement the defence policy; the way we are going to make the Canadian Forces be what Canada needs. Things don't keep me awake at night, but when I wake up at night I think about those things you have been talking about here. But if I thought only about problems, I would walk into the executive floor of National Defence Headquarters simply to use it as a springboard to commit seppuku. But I don't. I walk in there and I use those problems as a way to generate frustration and turn that frustration into rage, and turn that rage into cold, hard decisions so those problems will not defeat us.

Our defence policy talked about the changed political landscape, the threat, discussed the complex array of challenges in front of us from a security standpoint. The national security policy said that Canadians understand this new reality. How many people here actually believe that the threat has really changed, that it is going to impact the world, and that it could impact Canada directly, but will always impact us indirectly? I think Canadians still need to be educated about this.

Gen R J Hillier

I know we talk about failed and failing states a lot, but we do not see failed and failing states as the source of all evil in all cases. They do not necessarily cause terrorism; they are not necessarily the root

---

**General R. J. Hillier** is the Chief of Defence Staff.

cause of it either. What I do see is failed and failing states as being a fertile garden for the growth of things like terrorism. Terrorism can be incubated in such places - you can get recruits, protection, training and resources there. Operations can be planned and from there you can spread venom and violence the world over. Therefore if we address the challenges posed by failed and failing states we have a chance to neutralize or at least have a mitigating effect on terrorism.

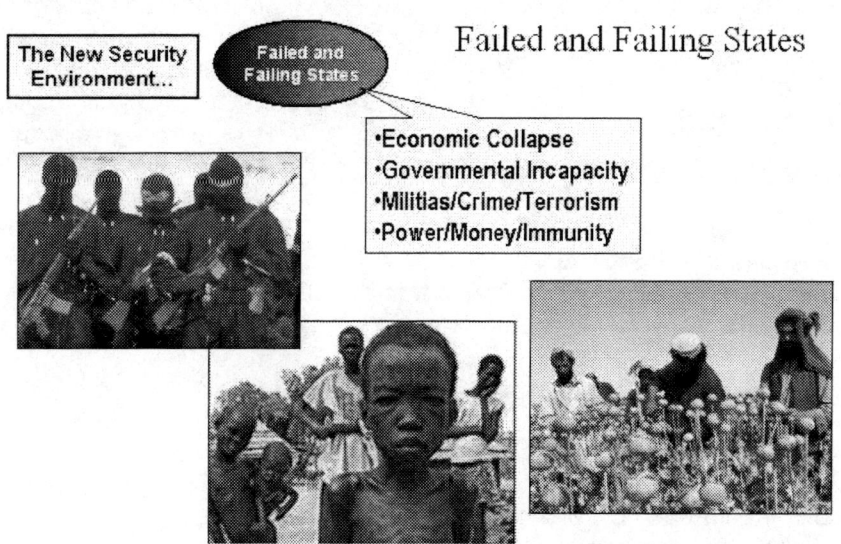

Organized crime is a perfect example of the ripple effects of state failure. It moved out of the Balkans in the mid-1990s after it had the opportunity to flourish there and went global. It now has an impact on our nation. My personal experience (and this is not official policy) is that all those individuals, scoundrels all of them, are after power. Power to dictate to people how they are going to live. Power to dictate whether women can live in a society freely, or if men can make democratic choices, or whether they have individual rights. They want money in order to gain more power.

Not all of them can be reasoned with. I use the example of the small city in Prijedor in Bosnia. A city of about 150,000-175,000 people that was multi-ethnic for hundreds and hundreds of years. During 1991-1992 we ended up with a situation in Prijedor were the mayor of the town was the equivalent of [serial killer] Clifford Olsen and the chief of police was [convicted murderer] Paul Bernardo and the chief of public security was [accomplice] Karla Homolka. Now you do not reason with folks like that; you have to deal with them from a position of strength. These are some of the challenges faced in failed and failing states.

All that I have to say is that the threat has changed. I like to use this slide to say the conventional threat on the left has now become a conventional threat on the

right (see left). We have gone from the Warsaw Pact-type of state player that threatens us to a ball of snakes. That ball of snakes is seen differently by many, and causes some discussion and sometimes dissention amongst otherwise friendly and cooperative allies, and countries that usually work together. So it is difficult to perceive a unifying fear such as the one NATO grappled with during the Cold War. When you have 26 nations in an institution like NATO, all of whom view that ball of snakes differently, it is hard to get that same consensus. That is one of the challenges that we have to work through.

The Warsaw Pact was our conventional threat. We structured, equipped, trained, educated, led and stationed ourselves against that. Nowadays that is the asymmetric threat and the ball of snakes is the conventional threat. And so we really are at the front end of a process, changing the way we structure, equip, train, educate, and in general prepare ourselves against this threat.

You want to talk of threats that show up and weapons of mass destruction? Let's start with Afghanistan and 4,000 tons of raw opium produced each year. There you have it - a weapon of mass destruction, albeit with a slightly longer fuse. I drove up a valley in the northeast part of Afghanistan that was nothing but one field after another; 90% of it going into Western Europe, 10% going into western North America including the port of Vancouver. You talk of weapons of mass destruction that flourish in a failed or failing state, this is it. And there is no easy solution to getting rid of it. Essentially you have to build a country before you can even start to crimp something like this.

When I say we now have to adapt to that ball of snakes, we are talking about being in support of and living amongst the people in these fragile countries. We want to keep them on side when we deploy. Our men and women have to keep a clear sense of this aspect of the mission. That requires a new level of confidence, education and training. We have to be very careful when operating in a place like Kosovo or Afghanistan that we have the right focus from their perspective and from the mission perspective. We can easily default to a mindset where the mission is about Canada or about NATO or about everything but those people inside Afghanistan. The minute we do, they start to reject our presence and our assistance, and they go from being friendly to neutral to hostile to trying to kill us in a heartbeat. Since that is not where we want to be, we must not lose sight of whom we're serving.

The stresses that living amongst a foreign population impose on the servicemen and women are pretty incredible. Among four million people in Kabul, 25-50 probably would want to kill you on a given day. Between 50 and 100 would probably be inclined to assist that 25-50, but four million wanted you there. If you went of the gate of Camp Julien as a Canadian soldier and treated all four million like that first group, by week three they would all be trying to kill you. So the professional standards we demand from those young men and women are pretty incredible.

The physical context is significant. Right now we are structured, prepared, and trained to avoid dense urban areas. On the North German Plain, with wide open areas, we are right at home. But not in the towns. We were always trained to prepare to bypass and isolate urban areas and let follow-on forces handle it. Starve them out, wait them out, but never fight through this objective. That is now where we conduct our operations. And none of our training, none of our equipment has been optimized to allow us to act effectively in three dimensions.

The last thing I will say is that we operated at that tactical level. But we also tried to translate all of those tactical operations into reasonable objectives that would help Afghanistan become that stable, democratic society that is part of a more stable region. Thus we operated at that very strategic level. We had a planning team that worked at the operational level, that went in to work for the government of Afghanistan to help them articulate their vision into strategy, plans and policies that would rebuild the country. So, on a daily basis we worked all three levels.

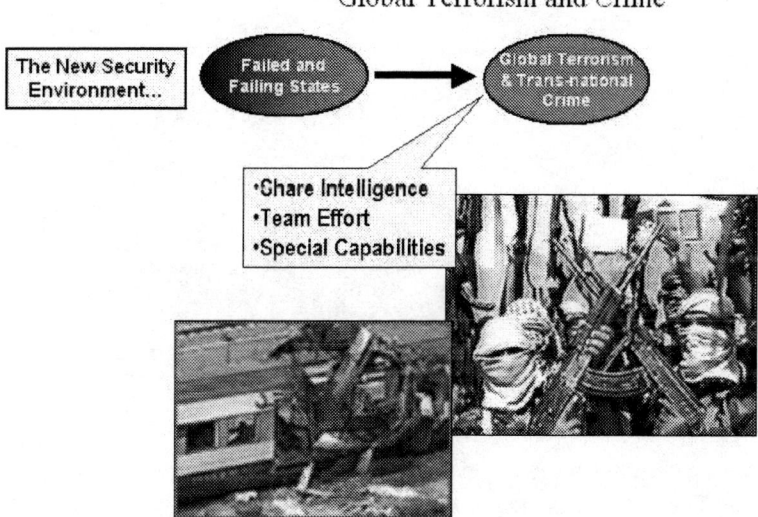

The importance of sharing intelligence cannot be understated. Having worked with many nations in the past, I can tell you that we have significant work to do to remove some of the protocols on information and intelligence sharing so as to obtain that common operating picture that will allow us to accomplish our mission.

I talk about team effort. I do not believe there is a thing such as an exclusively Canadian Forces mission. If Canada takes on a mission then we need to take it on in its entirety and go at it as the Canadian government. The Canadian Forces obviously have a part to play in that, but if you are just asking us to conduct security operations without simultaneously building the country around us - whether it is in Kosovo, Afghanistan or anywhere else - we really are setting ourselves up for failure. I think 3-D is a Canadian approach, a "Team Canada" approach, and we need the rest of the departments involved and we need private industry involved all at the same time.

Industry wants to come in and build our camps, support us, do our maintenance for us, and then 10 years later when everything is stabilized and secure it can establish a factory and continue to develop its business. We need industry there on day one. As we try to reduce militia forces, the sole impediment is always employment for the young men being demobilized. So we need industry to come with us on day one, take some risks with us on day one, support us and be supported as part of the team. Team Canada is a much better definition than 3-D, which has started well. However I think we have to go far beyond it.

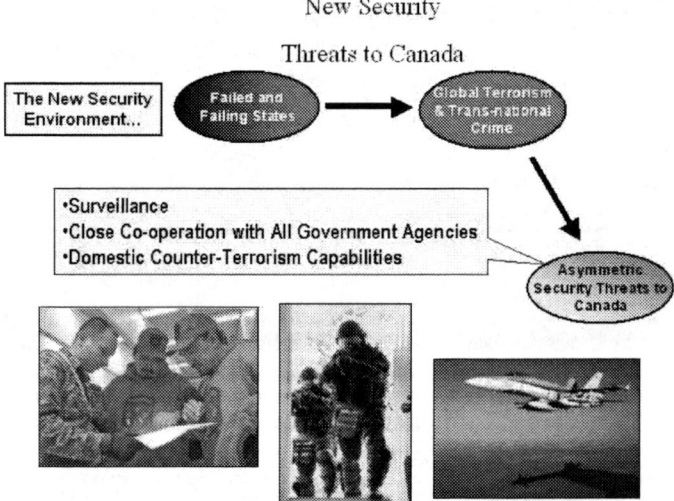

We are cooperating more closely with all agencies and departments across Canada. The Team Canada approach is just as urgently required at home as internationally. Building domestic counter-terrorist capabilities is key. You need those extremely capable and professional men and women to be able to prosecute operations either here in Canada or abroad, and so we are going to put in place the Special Operations Group (SOG) built around Joint Task Force 2 (JTF-2), but with additional capabilities resident in the infantry units that support JTF-2. This is a growth business because that is what's needed against the ball of snakes.

One other thing that we need to have is an operating picture common to all government players in the security equation. What we have brought together allows us to achieve a measure of all-domain awareness. What we want to do now is focus on integrated readiness. We need to view Canada as an operational theatre, ensuring that we have gone beyond simple force generation to force employment, achieving a level of readiness now that enables us to achieve our domestic tasks. The readiness of the Canadian Forces by and large has been measured against international operations. Except for the immediate reaction units and the NORAD commitments, all our readiness levels are tied to getting ready to go abroad. A significant chunk of the Canadian Forces - the majority, in fact - is not assessed as being prepared (or not) to respond to an event in Canada.

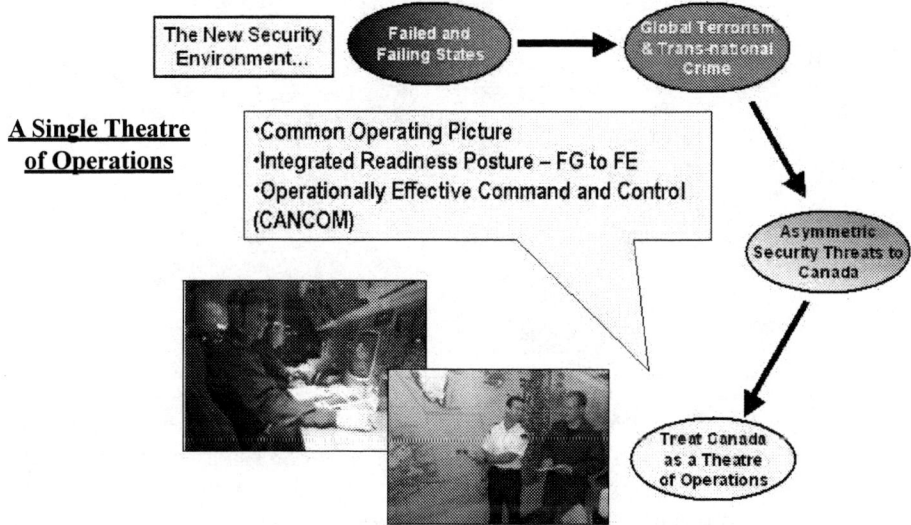

Lastly, command and control is a big piece of the puzzle. When we look at Canada as an operational theatre, we look at doing what we do in any other operational theatre. This means one commander and one command team with the authority, responsibility and accountability to conduct operations in Canada. By this I mean contingency operations in support of the Government of Canada, provincial governments, municipal governments and the first and second responders. We have established Canada Command (CANCOM), appointed a commander, and are establishing a command cadre. We have established the first of the joint task forces in Atlantic Canada under CANCOM and they are already starting to conduct operations. We are going to learn from Joint Task Force Atlantic over the next six months, and then we are going to reproduce those lessons. We are going to have one commander with six regional commanders, who has first call on every man, woman and piece of equipment in that region to conduct operations. In Atlantic Canada we have 19 separate lines of command going into Halifax. We are going to reduce that down to about two. In fact we are going to reduce it down to one for operations. There will be some significant changes in that we will have an effective command and control system.

What I want CANCOM to do is to run operations, to develop the contingency plans to respond to natural or man-made disasters, in the most effective way possible. It will not to act as a first responder, but will be able to support those first responders and then to exercise those plans in conjunction with the rest of Team Canada.

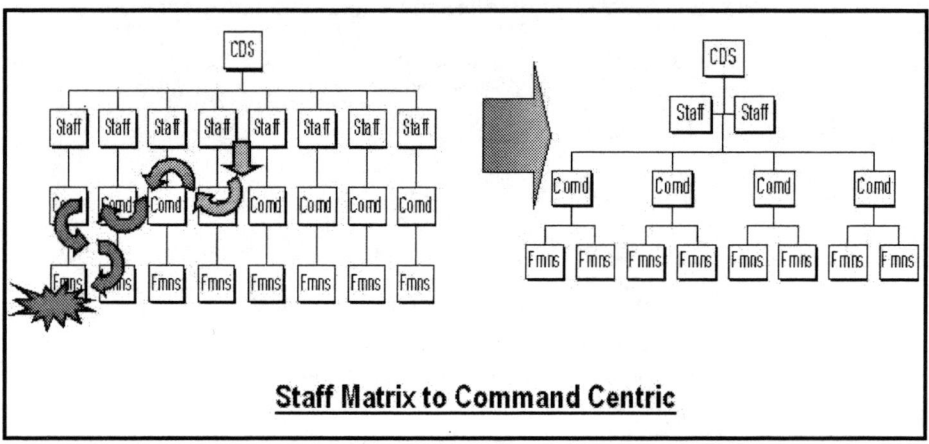

**Staff Matrix to Command Centric**

One of the things we are going to do is move now to a command-centric system from a staff matrix (see above). The CDS is the commander of the Canadian Forces who operates at the strategic level, supplying strategic guidance, supported by a small joint staff, working to four operational commanders who will be responsible for the conduct of operations. These are:

1. Commander of CANCOM who will run operations in Canada;

2. Commander of Canadian Expeditionary Forces Command (CEFCOM) who will have responsibility for international operations;

3. Commander of the special operations group who will have all the spe-

cial operation forces under his or her command, and will either conduct operations alone, or will provide the capability to the other two commanders;

4. A Joint Support Command which will provide the operational support directly to those other three commanders. Each of those commanders will be supported by a small command team.

We are not adding redundancies here; we are cutting this piece out of the National Defence Headquarters and the overhead we have built into that staff matrix, so that at the end of the day, for those here who know the organization, the Deputy Chief of Defence Staff (DCDS) group will disappear. Huge changes to the Associate Deputy Minister (Human Resources-Military) group, and changes right across Assistant Deputy Minister portfolios will result. Where it makes sense, some of the staffs will be separated into military and civilian. Where it makes practical sense, combined and integrated staffs will continue to exist.

The second major priority for us is the continental defence picture. We believe there is room for NORAD to foster situational awareness in all domains - including the maritime domain. But as we seek to build the right relationship with the United States (my part of it being the military piece) it is critical that what we do is always seen as credible by our partner to the south. What we do here gives us far more buy-in and credibility and profile than almost anything we do elsewhere. What we do externally, in an expeditionary context, is secondary.

On the international expeditionary side, we are standing up CEFCOM, and we are going to stand up the standing contingency task force, which I want to have as the Canadian Forces' contribution to rapid response. It will be based on a light unit organization of about 1,000 army personnel, supported by a naval task group, with the appropriate aviation capability, under one commander, which can be brought to full readiness within ten days of a notice to move. It becomes the first responder internationally. Then it depends on how long it is out there whether we rotate another such unit into the theatre of operations or repatriate it and put it back into readiness mode.

The key is to achieve a focused effect. To achieve the desired effect we need to keep the smaller operations to the minimum, and to focus our human and material resources in a way that give us the footprint, profile, credibility, and the leadership opportunities to allow us to shape regions like Afghanistan in accordance with our interest and/or values.

The three-block war looms large in all of this. If you are knocking something down in the conduct of operations, you had better be building the country up as you are doing it or you are wasting your time. You need to build a police force, an army, and generally step in to fill a void if other things are not being done.

The key question is, what is the strategy? What are you trying to achieve when Canada commits to a place like Afghanistan? What is the plan to enhance governance and security and to develop social capital, rebuild your infrastructure, and establish the rule of law and a justice system? The campaign plan has to be clearly articulated as we go out the door. Once that is laid out, how do you then put your budgetary process against it? How do you get the international community to finance it?

When you talk about the role of our provincial reconstruction team (PRT) in Afghanistan, these are the issues we're dealing with at the provincial level. We are trying to build the capacity of the government of Kandahar province. The governor and his team there need help to shape that investment strategy to rebuild Kandahar. We must carefully consider how to get the international community to support that effort, as well as how it should be supported by our military forces at a time the latter are helping to train indigenous security forces. In the past, we, the Canadian military, did not pay particular attention to the strategic effect because we have always handed troops off to other people to command. We are past that now and want to achieve some very specific effects.

Let me re-emphasize the fact that our business is still a hard-nosed business. We have got to be able to do all the other [non-combat] jobs, but the hard stuff is why we exist. And as I say, when you have a Clifford Olsen, a Paul Bernardo and a Karla Holmolka, sometimes the hard stuff is required. Certainly the threat of force it is almost always required in some of those places until you establish your own indigenous governance and security capabilities.

But we are not succeeding in driving that strategic aspect home. I have to look those young men and women right in the eye, and when one of them comes home in a body bag, and we cannot articulate why that sacrifice was necessary, then we have failed them. That is not where we want to be. I am not talking policy, I am talking about my responsibility as Chief of Defence Staff to explain to intelligent young men and women who ask me why we are doing this. You must tell them what we are aiming for, what is the expected effect going to be five years out, why they are here right now, and why they are accepting this risk. You cannot say they are being sent somewhere just because they are professional soldiers.

Back to my first point about supporting people on a mission, you also need to convince Afghans that you are going to have some positive effect several years down the road. They understand you are not going to change in several months what occurred over the course of several years. They have the patience and have said to us a number of times, "We know it is going to take 10, 15, 20 years, but if you convince me now that what we are all doing together, or what you are doing 15 years from now will make a better place here for my child, then I will put up with anything for the next 15 years." But you need to be able to walk them through that strategy. You have to be able to tell them what we are doing, why we are doing it and the effect we are going to get from it.

You had also better be able to justify it to the families of those who are serving. I have pinned enough Silver Crosses on widows and mothers in these past years that I have to tell you, when I send young men and women out of the country I would just like to make sure they know why they are going and what they are going to achieve.

Let me just talk very briefly about the principles I put in place after I talked to my commanders in Cornwall, Ontario in June. These principles will guide us and assist the Canadian Forces in implementing transformation.

### New CF Operational Focus

*Outer elements (clockwise from top):* Failed and Failing States; Global Terrorism & Trans-national Crime; Asymmetric Security Threats to Canada; Treat Canada as a Theatre of Operations; Credible Domestic & Continental Security; Focused Full Spectrum Expeditionary Capabilities.

*Ring:* CEFCOM / CANCOM

**PRINCIPLES**
- CF Culture
- Operations Primacy
- Command-Centric
- Mission Command
- Responsibility, Authority & Accountability
- Regular, Reserve & Civilian

*A CF-wide culture and attitude.* Wrapping the fundamental pillars of the air, land and sea forces into a Canadian Forces context will guide our people toward what they have to achieve and how they are going to do it. No need for transformation to take place separately by service. A joint attitude will filter down to operational entities. When we put that standing contingency task force out the door we are going to be wanting to shape the mission, so that operational entity of air, land and sea assets stays together under Canadian command. I think perhaps for too long we have just handed forces off to allies to employ, and they have always wanted just a bit of army, a bit of navy, and a bit of air force. As a result our contributions have always been just below the radar scope, and we never got, I think, full credit for it.

*Operational primacy versus institutional protection.* Over the last 10-12 years we have faced high stress in operations and a significant cut in resources - the worst combination imaginable. I think all of our branches went into self-protection mode and created fences - whether it was the artillery branch, the armoured branch or the infantry branch inside of the army, or the army inside of the CF or the navy inside of the CF. Now we have to get back to focusing on the operational dimension because success on operations is what we will be measured by. Hence we have got to make sure that everything (structures, equipment, etc.) is going to enable us.

*New mission command philosophy.* I talked about being command-centric, and that what we have to do to make that a reality: asking people to achieve something and giving them guidance, but not telling them exactly what to do. And then giving them the responsibility, authority and accountability along with the resources to go and do it.

I am going start summing up here by telling you that in regards to transformation, we have been at it for about six or seven years. I would say that 99 percent of the transformational efforts in Western militaries has been focused on the high-intensity fight. So transformation only now is starting to realize what that ball of snakes actually means. We are just starting the transformational process here despite the work that has gone on over this past while.

The last thing I will say is this is a uniquely Canadian approach here. What does Canada need? How relevant are we going to be to Canadians so they will support us in the future, so they see themselves in us, and so that they see us as a fundamental part of Canadian society? We have got to be relevant to them, and this new approach is the way to achieve that.

# QUESTION & ANSWER FORUM

**David Rudd, CISS**

General, there are a number of trap doors which lie underneath the plans for the defence policy's implementation. Can we just talk briefly about human and material resources? No transformation will take place without the right people and the right number of people. What can the recruiting system do to get those extra 5,000 regulars and 3,000 reservists into service as quickly as possible? As for material resources, is it within the capability of DND to shorten the procurement process or does that lie completely outside your and DND's span of control?

**General Rick Hillier**

Let me talk about the human resources dimension a bit. First, we have great men and women; second, we need to focus their efforts very precisely. We still have not figured out how to fit 30 hours into a 24-hour day, so we need to focus them. We need to ensure that the tasks we are undertaking have been prioritized, that they fit within the transformation paradigm, and that operations come first. I believe we can do that by employing the command-centric approach.

Sometimes we do take on a bit of a victimization attitude; we say we are much too busy, or that we can't possibly do anything else. But when you peel away the layers of the onion, the priorities of some of the things that we are doing just need to be re-assessed.

In terms of recruiting, it is true we have not marketed ourselves in an aggressive manner. But we have still met our goal of some 4,000 recruits coming through our door. We want to recruit an additional 8,000 kids, and we do want kids! The youth are without question the lifeblood of an army, navy and air force. We take them at all ages obviously, but I prefer the youth to come in. We believe there are significant untapped markets out there, and we realise the need to better reflect the demographic of our country. We need to reflect our country's population. We have a population of various ethnic communities across our country comprising two million or more in various groups. We have not made any in-roads into most of these communities. We have a chance to tap into those sources and say, hey, we offer adventure, we offer an opportunity to be part of something greater than yourself, and we offer benefits and pay that are competitive with any organization or industry, and we offer you a chance to be part of the Canadian Forces.

As to the question of material resources, before I criticize anybody outside the department I'd like to look inside and sort ourselves out. First, there is a responsibility for me, as Chief of Defence Staff, and with the advice of the Armed Forces Council, to define for those big, transformational equipments what the requirements are. I'm not talking about 15,000 pages of specification. I'm saying when we need a helicopter or aircraft, or a fighting vehicle or a ship I am going to articulate four to six key principles - lines in the sand, if you will - that will become the driving force in the acquisition process. We have not tended to do that in the past, and when I said I was going to do this in April at NDHQ it sent a shudder through the building and through the staff. But that's my job, and I need advice to help shape it, but I'm going to do that. So for a helicopter, I'll say that I need to lift this much, at this altitude, this temperature, over this distance.

Second, we will have to take an appetite suppressant for the Canadianization of equipment. If we buy a fighting vehicle from somewhere other than Canada, then the only thing we should be changing on it is where we put the communication systems. If it is good enough that we have decided to buy it, then we buy it as is.

Third, I have great concerns on how we approach the acquisition process. I am reluctant to buy a paper anything. I have concerns first with the Canadian Forces, but I am now more aware of the impact on Canadian industry as well. But I am not in the risk business. If I have a billion dollars and I am buying helicopters, or if I have two billion dollars, I want as many and as much capability as I can get for that two billion, as opposed to using 25 percent of that to generate regional benefits. So we have the money, and I think we can speed the acquisition process ourselves.

If we are grappling with a 12-year acquisition cycle, I would like to identify the requirement 10-12 years before we need the item and start the acquisition process, as opposed to wait until we need the item and start the 12-year acquisition cycle. I think also that the political considerations needs to be resolved up front, and I think this is possible with an active defence minister like Bill Graham.

**Sunil Ram**

General, one of the greatest disconnects in Canada has been the civil-military relationship. That is an inability of the military, and possibly the politicians, to understand the needs and requirements of the Canadian Forces. I think this may be one of the greatest stumbling blocks that you face. One is left with the impression that there is not an understanding by the public, or at least a clear understanding, of the type of danger we face. In this venue you are preaching to the converted. The question is, is the message getting to those politicians who can make those decisions down the line?

**Gen Hillier**

There are many ways to communicate, and clearly a small percentage of that comes through me. The rest comes through the great society in which we live and I think it has to come to the population at large to have an effect. But I do see the Canadian population right now, in general, waking from their slumber.

We have to reach out. As a mission, we have to connect with the citizenry in every demographic group. We have to treat this as a mission. This is a mission for CANCOM, and must be conducted in a very operational and focused way.

I was at the opening weekend of the Calgary Stampede, where we had some excellent pieces of the Canadian Forces on display to show who we are, what we do and what we mean to the country. We had the crew of HMCS *Calgary*, who have a great relationship with the city, the army gun race team, a contingent of soldiers from the last ISAF rotation, and a Griffon helicopter flying the flag as it passed the grandstand. The entire Stampede Committee and Spruce Meadows Jumping Committee and the City of Calgary wanted to promote the Canadian Forces. While we were out there, the Snowbirds were flying elsewhere in the country, the Sky Hawks parachute team was elsewhere in the country, and we had CF-18s were flying elsewhere in the country. But we were missing the opportunity to appeal to 1.4 million people in a concentrated area. So we are giving CANCOM a mission. We are going to concentrate on six annual events across the country: Carnival in Quebec City, the Nova Scotia Tattoo, Canada Day in Ottawa, the Canadian National Exhibition in Toronto, the Pacific National Exhibition in Vancouver, and the Calgary Stampede. We are going to have a Canadian Forces operation to participate, raise our profile, be out there, and connect with the people. The last thing we did not have at the Stampede was a recruiting vendor. We had all these people coming through, all sorts of young men and women who we'd like to talk to, but no capability to engage them.

We have to connect with the population, and it cannot just be me. It has to be those 62,500 regular force members and the 24,000 reservist men and women. They have to go out and do it, but you have to help us and be our advocates and our spokesmen and women. That is the only way things will change.

**Bruce Taylor**

I'm one of several businesspeople here today. It's our stock in trade to be able to appeal to our consumers; to tell them what the benefits of our products are. There is a possibility, if you cared to avail yourself of it, of gathering together a committee of volunteers who might be able to explore new ways of thinking in terms of how we approach the average Canadian and win their hearts and minds in support of the value and importance of the military.

**Gen Hillier**

Every day I curse the fact that I do not have a thousand clones that I could pile on to issues like that because there is such enormous potential in it. Tom Ring, our assistant Deputy Minister for Public Affairs, has come in with a new look at how we can connect with Canadians, and he views his job as telling the Canadian Forces story. This is the first time in my career that I have heard anything like from the public affairs side, and we are actually looking at all the ways we can do that. John Eaton runs our Canadian Forces Liaison Council, which includes the businessmen and women who are specifically focused on the Canadian Forces. The Council was established to consider how we could best support the reserves, but it has clearly become more than that.

I would like to take you up on the offer. I would like you to actually pull together a group and be able to brainstorm this and see where we can use the men and women from the private sector to be able to help Canadians be more aware of what their armed forces are, what they do, what great citizens they are, how they represent them around the world, and how much their service actually really does mean.

**Khanh Lekim, CISS Member**

I came here to support the Canadian Forces and your role. I am very proud, although I am not a military man. You have performed a wonderful job for all of us - not only for Canada, but for the whole world. And I come here to give you my support and thank you very much for your service.

**Gen Hillier**

Thank you. I think there are many things that are tough, but with those problems there is an awesome opportunity to actually take the Canadian Forces higher, to build on what has been so well guarded and kept intact. When I look around this room and see many people, people who came through the very toughest of times, I realise that in fact the CF survived, even if it was not by much. We did not survive by much given the huge demands on us as budgets were going down. But I look around and see people who have gone before and have given us the conditions for change. We have talked about a lot of things here today, and all or some of the ideas that have come up are on track. But we still have a lot of work to do.

**Unidentified Speaker**

Building on one of the previous speaker's comments regarding use of reserves, one of our biggest problems is getting reserves free for the better part of nine months for a deployment; to leave their jobs or whatever they are doing, to put their lives on hold for nine months to go off and support the regular force. Is there a strategy in place or in development where we can seek support from the business community so they will allow their people to go off and then come back to the jobs they left?

**Gen Hillier**

I think the strategy is in place; it is just how aggressively we pursue it. I will go back to the example in the United States where job protection is in place. I had the good fortune of working with the Texas National Guard's 49th Lone Star Division for about 18-24 months, helping to prepare them for their mission in Bosnia, which was an 18-month operation. I was quite interested in how the job protection legislation worked. First of all, when they had to use the legislation to protect one of their soldiers, they regarded it as an operational or strategic failure. They had not done their salesmanship in connecting with that business or company or organization and convincing them of what that soldier, NCO or officer, going off to train, going to Bosnia and coming back, would bring to the company. So they regarded it as a failure, but at the end of the day it was a safety net. One time they had used it, and the Houston Independent School District was fined $865,000 for refusing to allow a teacher - a senior NCO - to partake in the operation and that acted as an example for everyone else. I think there is an opportunity to offer better protection to young Canadians who want to serve their country through the Canadian Forces and not have to pay an extra cost.

**Peter Hunter, Reserves 2000**

I have an observation and then a question. First, regarding the mix of people in the military and the proper representation of diversity in Canada, I think there are two sides to that particular equation. The reserves, I think, represent us very well. In fact in some units it is hard to find someone who can speak English. At the other end of that extreme, the regular forces do not reflect this. My question is, you talk about a Canadian Forces culture, but do you think that people out there can relate to the Canadian Forces?

**Gen Hillier**

What we have to do for the demographic dimension is balance the Canadian Forces. We have to reflect our country and when someone looks at us they have to see themselves in us. Right now, not every Canadian can. But we will never be perfect.

Can people relate to the Canadian Forces? I try to put it this way to them: I am proud, I am a soldier, I am proud that I am a dragoon. But lets not be so foolish with our pride that we constrain ourselves to silos. Let's be proud that we are Canadians. I have talked to probably 20,000 people in the Canadian Forces directly in the past six months about this, and they respond incredibly; the young men and women at the junior rank level even more so than any of the others. They understand that we are all involved in every mission. No mission is unique to a service, no mission is uniquely Canadian, no mission is uniquely military and no mission is uniquely a secret. So we are joint and we are combined and we are multi-agency and we are public in every mission we undertake. They recognize that and they can relate to it.

**Lin Armstrong Sharwood, CEO, Spirit of Success Inc.**

I represent a water purification and energy company. I started a year ago to work with the Minister of National Defence and the head of procurement. I was told at the beginning of the year that it would probably take about eight years before someone in the military would ever see our product. The military made it clear that they would like a demonstration of the products we offer, but the personnel I was corresponding with on the procurement side did not know how to arrange the demonstration. So the military was telling me to bring the product into the procurement department, but the people who were actually in the department did not really know what the procedures were for following through with this. So there are all these disconnects that make it difficult for the private sector to contribute to the national defence effort.

One way these disconnects could be overcome would be to adopt an approach similar to the United States. In 2000, the United States Army invited women from all over the world to come to Washington and partake in a trade show to demonstrate how women could do business with the military. From this event, they produced a list of over 4,000 women's organizations that had come together to do business with the US military. I would be willing to become involved in transferring this type of model to Canada.

The other thing that I just want to point out, I am well over 50 years old.

**Gen Hillier**

You can still join! We do not have an age limit anymore.

**Lin Armstrong Sharwood**

You were speaking earlier about recruiting young people and their enthusiasm, and I thought again of most of the areas where reconstruction actually takes place. Women are vital to that reconstruction process, yet it is primarily men that are doing the organizing and planning. I am just going to say again that sometimes those of us that are over 50 or over 40 or over 30 might have some really great ideas from our experience that we could impart. Even though we might have been at home raising our children and might be over 40 or 50 when we rejoin the workforce, we can still be a valuable asset. So that is another way of implementing your plan.

**Gen Hillier**

Thank you very much for that. You will remember all the fuss back in the 1980s about whether or not we would allow women in the military in any capacity other than as clerks and cooks. I remember thinking at the time how I had grown up in a family with five sisters - four of whom were older than me - and no bothers. Everyday I got beat up by one of those girls. So there was never doubt in my mind ever whatsoever that we were going to have women as a full part of the Canadian Forces.

I wish I was able to talk to you about the first two points in detail. I cannot, but we are sure trying to make life a little better in terms of how we do business. Again, I wish I could clone myself a thousand times to personally handle each of those issues, but in the interim I have got a lot of fine officers, NCOs and soldiers who can do that.

**Glen Dean**

Do you consider the consequences for Canada of an escalated war footing? We are at war, we need to defend our allies, we need to defeat bin Laden's *fatwa*, and we also have our own country to defend. So will you be keeping an eye on the future of Canada as a nation as we go forward?

**Gen Hillier**

To this I would prescribe a uniquely Canadian approach. I am a proud Canadian. I am the most proud Canadian I can be because I love our country. I love everything about our country, including some of the things I do not like about our country. I was telling our prime minister one day that democracy, at times, is much easier to defend than it is to understand or work within. But that is the great strength of our country.

I went on ceremonial guard duty on Parliament Hill on July 21, 2005 and I drilled with the Old Guard, all of whom were young French-Canadian soldiers out of Montreal. What an incredible energy they bring to the Canadian Forces and to our country. How proud they were to do it, how proud they were to do it in their maternal language, and how great it was for myself to go out and participate with them. From my perspective, as we deploy around the world to operational theatres, the fact that almost all of our officers, many of our NCOs, and a huge chunk of our soldiers can speak a minimum of two languages becomes an incredible force multiplier. This is true when working inside of NATO, working inside of ISAF, working in Kosovo, and working with the United Nations. It is quite incredible what an enabler this provides.

I am a proud Canadian. I love this country and would not want to see anything happen to it except to see it strengthened, and I will play a part in that anywhere I possibly can.

**Colonel Joel Wolfe, CISS Member**

At the end of 1945, about 90 percent of battalion commanders in the Canadian army were members of the militia or graduates of the Officer Training Corps (OTC) units at their universities. The Canadian army reserves were actually the most important element in the leadership of our fighting troops at the end of the war. With that as a guide, and as a symbol, I am asking you if anything can be done to simplify the recruiting process which is hampering the enlargement and the success of the few militia regiments that are still active in Canada?

**Gen Hillier**

To begin with, I will tell you that an enormous number of steps have been taken on three or four fronts regarding this. One is reducing the amount of time involved in the recruiting process. One of the things that causes a significant delay from the time a individual walks into a recruiting centre to the time they are actually enrolled in the reserves is the medical sign-off verifying they are medically fit. The physician's assistant conducts the actual assessment but this needs to be signed off by a senior medical officer in Ottawa. This sign-off process often took three months or more. When we conducted an assessment we found that 99 percent of all individuals assessed were subsequently approved by the senior medical officer. Our question was, could we not accept this one percent risk factor? Could we not enrol these individuals right away subject to the medical officer's review? We have done that.

One of the challenges I gave to ADM-HR (Mil) was to change the component transfer time - reserve to regular, and regular to reserve. I told him I wanted to reduce the time it takes a soldier to go from the reserve component to the regular force, which up until last week was 22 weeks. I said I wanted that to be one week, Monday to Friday. He came back to me with all the measures in place for a four-week transfer. So I took the four weeks as an interim deal and we will go from there. But I also want this to work the other way - regular to reserve - as well.

We recruit young women with the intention of having lots of them as part of our force, because without them we cannot have the force size we need. About 4-6 years in, these young women, many of whom go into the combat arms, are into ages where they find a partner and many of them have families. And what they instantly discover is that they cannot balance the demands we place on them in full-time service with a family life; the only recourse they have right now is to take their release. Thus we lose a multi-million dollar, multi-year investment. What I want is to be able to do is to effortlessly slide a young woman from the regular component to the reserve component; to be able to offer her that option, let her go on a Class A service so that she can balance her family life. When she is ready to return to full-time service, even if it is 6-8 years later when the kids are in school, she has the option to carry on with her career. In this way we realize the investment we have put into her.

So it is not just the recruiting part. A whole variety of things that need to change, and we are expending massive resources to improve them. Kevin Cotton, the new commander of the Canadian Forces Recruiting Group, needs to be commended by a whole bunch of people in both the reserve and the regular components for the work he's done to minimize some of the frustrations that we have had to deal with.